Dear Grandpa —

You're my champion.

Love,

Doug

a

to

Bill Parcells

with

Jeff Coplon

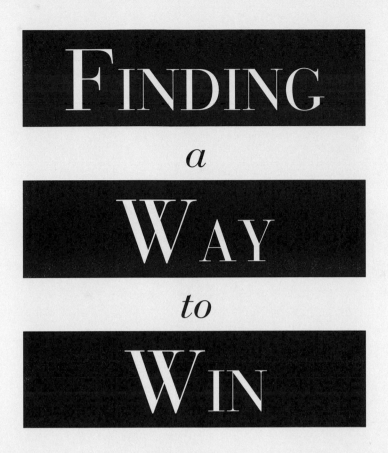

FINDING a WAY to WIN

The Principles of Leadership,
Teamwork, and Motivation

D O U B L E D A Y
New York London Toronto Sydney Auckland

PUBLISHED BY DOUBLEDAY
a division of Bantam Doubleday Dell Publishing Group, Inc.
1540 Broadway, New York, New York 10036

DOUBLEDAY and the portrayal of an anchor with a dolphin
are trademarks of Doubleday, a division of
Bantam Doubleday Dell Publishing Group, Inc.

Library of Congress Cataloging-in-Publication Data

Parcells, Bill.
Finding a way to win : the principles of leadership, teamwork, and
motivation / Bill Parcells with Jeff Coplon. — 1st ed.
        p.   cm.
1. Football—Coaching—Philosophy.   2. Teamwork (Sports)
    3. Leadership.   4. Work groups.   I. Coplon, Jeff.
                II. Title.
            GV954.4.P37   1995
796.322'07'7—dc20   95-35476
                                                              CIP

ISBN 0-385-48122-5

1   3   5   7   9   10   8   6   4   2

To all the great players I've been fortunate to coach who once were able to call themselves champions;

And to Mickey Corcoran, the guy who will always be my coach.

—B.P.

To Milt, who has inspired so many with his confidence, humility, and resourcefulness—and who understands that winning is a process.

—J.C.

ACKNOWLEDGMENTS

The authors would like to thank David Gernert, the Doubleday publisher who first imagined this book; Bill Thomas, our ever vigilant and supportive editor; our hard-working agents, Robert Fraley and Michael Carlisle, along with Richard Neal of Leader Enterprises; Don Lowery and Stacey James of the New England Patriots' public relations staff; and Aaron Salkin, public relations assistant for the New York Giants.

CONTENTS

a

to

Prologue

THE NARCOTIC
of WINNING

A NUMBER OF YEARS AGO, DURING MY TIME AS HEAD COACH OF the New York Giants, my wife and I were relaxing in our living room, shortly before the start of another football season. It was just a typical, quiet evening, until Judy asked me: "Why do you continue to do this job? What kind of ego makes you bring this on yourself again? You're always so miserable— most of the time you're anxious, or exasperated, or depressed. What is it that makes you do this?"

I couldn't answer her; I couldn't explain myself. All the logic was on Judy's side. A coach lives in a black and white world—you win or you lose—and the black side stays with you a lot longer.

I had some wonderful years with those Giants. When you can field a team with people like Phil Simms and Lawrence Taylor and Mark Bavaro and Bart Oates, you exude confidence. You've got the trump cards. Though you know you might lose, it will take a hell of a team to beat you.

But there have been other years when my teams were

mediocre, or worse. I've spent whole seasons buried in frustration. Not because we didn't work hard enough, or try hard enough, or exploit the talent on hand. Most of the time we did all of those things, but we still *lost*, and that's all that mattered.

And even when you have a good team, the odds are pretty strong that you'll wind up on the dark side. There are thirty head coaches in the NFL, and twenty-nine of them will trudge home as losers at the end of the season, regardless of how much they achieved along the way.

To get back to my wife's question: Why do I put up with this life? I guess it comes down to this: *Because it feels so good when you win.*

I think the same holds true for any job with heavy stress, high expectations, and grinding competition—in other words, for the greater part of our business world. Whether you're a sales rep, or an account executive, or a factory manager, you're under the gun. You're pushing to reach a goal—and if you're really good at what you do, the toughest goals are the ones you set yourself.

When you reach that goal, when you achieve at the highest level, there is tremendous satisfaction. We all strive to be recognized as one of the best in our field. It's no small accomplishment to get there—it demands effort and stamina far beyond the norm.

But there's a catch. The quest that we're on is impossible to complete. Because once you win, you've got to win all the time—and no one wins all the time. The world doesn't work that way.

As a coach, the most exciting days are when your team

plays well in a hotly contested game and pulls it out at the end. As that clock ticks down, and you know you've won, and your players start to celebrate, you're overcome by this wildly stimulating, euphoric sensation.

But the rush never lasts long. An hour or two later you're evaluating your team doctor's report, and very seldom is it clean. Even minor injuries can disrupt your preparation for the next game, and the major ones will force you to replace a player. The shadows begin to creep in, and soon that spectacular, soul-filling victory is yesterday's news.

Winning the Super Bowl is the ultimate pinnacle for a football coach. But if you have a real engine inside you, even that satisfaction can't be final; it creates an insatiable desire to do it again. Bobby Knight, who's scaled the mountaintop a few times himself, told me that I'd want to win my second championship a lot more than I wanted the first one. I found out he was right, and that it only gets worse. Because after we won the second one, I *really* wanted to win a third.

That desire goes beyond the scoreboard, or the fame, or the money. Those are just the incidentals, the by-products of winning. For me the point is something else: Can you contribute to greatness? Can you witness—even if just for a moment—an end product that reflects character and courage and principle?

Every winner I've met shares this craving to be the best. By itself, however, wanting it isn't enough. You need tools to lead your team to victory. *You need to find a way to win.* In this book we'll look at the building blocks of leadership, motivation, and teamwork. Using my experience in football as a framework, we'll explore how winners develop a vision and enlist others to join them; how they can enable those people to act, yet still direct the group's course; how they must model the way themselves, every step.

Leadership is a hot commodity these days. All around you'll find people selling the latest in armchair psychology or jargon-heavy motivational formulas. But there are no magic potions for success. The long-haul winners, the ones who last at the top in any organization, use a firmer foundation for success. They rely on old-fashioned things we call "values." That's the way we've organized this book—around values like candor and loyalty, patience and accountability, self-discipline and resourcefulness.

If we're to face the challenges of today's business world, and then to surmount them, we'll need those time-tested values more than ever before.

1.

INTEGRITY

To get to any destination worth reaching, you better have a road map. You better know *where* you're going—and *how* you're going to get there.

When organizations refer to "systems" or "philosophies," they're talking about the same thing. Scratch any thriving organization—it could be an electronics company, a law firm, or a football team—and you'll find a definite philosophy. These success stories have *integrity;* they stick to their organizational principles.

What some people fail to realize is that *it makes no difference what that philosophy is,* as long as it meets these standards:

THE PHILOSOPHY HAS A SOUND BASIC STRUCTURE.

IT REFLECTS THE LEADER'S VISION AND VALUES.

IT IS COMMUNICATED AND ACCEPTED THROUGHOUT THE ORGANIZATION.

MOST IMPORTANT, IT REMAINS IN PLACE LONG ENOUGH TO ALLOW FOR SUCCESS.

When leaders have a vision, they can picture the desired result of a project before they begin; they rely on their own measuring stick. When I put a new play in our offense, I know what it's supposed to look like before I tell my team about it.

And when organizations stay the course and hold fast to their philosophy, through good times and bad, they work from a firm foundation. They gain an identity. They *stand* for something.

Take Wal-Mart. From its start, this discount chain staked its future on supercompetitive pricing and aggressive, high-volume buying practices. It also generated high-level employee involvement, by enabling workers to gain shares in the company and have a personal stake in Wal-Mart profits. Product lines have come and gone in these stores, and competitors as well, but the Wal-Mart philosophy has stayed intact, and the company is going strong.

In the National Football League, philosophies start with the coach. The good ones all have a distinct approach to the game.

When Bill Walsh coached the 49ers, he liked to gain control by putting points on the board early; when he did, he became even more aggressive. While Walsh was ultra-creative on offense, and his teams liked to improvise, their structure was generally low risk and highly calculated.

Don Shula's greatest team, the 1972 Dolphins, was ground-oriented, with a selective—but explosive—passing game. His Dan Marino teams execute a more reckless game plan, but Shula remains efficient, prepared, the ultimate taskmaster.

Tom Landry was a cold thinking machine, totally unpredictable, and tremendously innovative over the course of his career. He was a bit of a gambler, and the best clock manager I'd ever seen.

When Jimmy Johnson came to the Cowboys, he built a big, powerful offense and an athletic, speed-oriented defense —just the opposite of a typical Landry team. Two Super Bowls later, the Johnson philosophy turned out to be equally effective.

Joe Gibbs taught a simple, powerful running game, along with solid, low-risk passing. His Redskin teams took their risks on defense. They were fundamentally sound and rarely beat themselves.

Buddy Ryan is a very dangerous coach. He tries to control the game with an aggressive, physical, heavy-blitzing defense; if you didn't block his defensive front in Philadelphia, you'd lose. I like Ryan's single-minded attitude. If he were given enough resources, and some patience within his organization, I think he could win at the highest level.

What do all these coaches have in common? They believe in themselves, and in their idea of how the game should be played. They don't cave in to pressure, or waver after temporary setbacks. They forge ahead.

A sustained philosophy doesn't guarantee victory, of course. Under Mike Holmgren, the Green Bay Packers have yet to gather the experience and talent to challenge the very top teams. But there's no doubt that Green Bay is playing to its potential, or that it's being guided with a sure hand. As long as Holmgren is head coach, the Packers will be a threat.

And I don't think it's a coincidence that the most successful franchise of the last fifteen years, the San Francisco 49ers, is also the one with the most stable and committed leadership. Eddie DeBartolo, the team's owner, has done everything necessary to succeed. He gave total support to Walsh, and then, after Walsh left, to a man with a similar approach, George Seifert. The team wins—and wins, and wins—because its philosophy is deeply rooted.

You could say the same thing about the NBA's Los Angeles Lakers under Jerry West and Jerry Buss.

The other great example is Don Shula, who's kept the Dolphins at or near the top for a quarter century. He's averaged more than ten victories per season over a thirty-two-year career, which is just remarkable. Don Shula is a guy with *integrity*—a guy who stays true to his values.

Would the Dolphins have fared as well over the last quarter century without that continuity on the sidelines? I think it's highly unlikely. You can't sustain excellence if you vacillate. In any business there are natural ebbs and flows. When organizations panic during the downturns, when they're in a constant state of flux, when they repeatedly turn over their management—those are the ones you don't have to worry about beating.

Let's say you're in a seasonal business, a travel agency, which has prospered with a philosophy of customer service.

After several years of steady growth, one summer your bookings are down 10 percent.

What do you do now? Fire half your agents and terrify the rest? Cut back on costs by compromising your service standards?

The smarter manager looks at all the factors—Was the weather worse this year? Did airlines raise their fares? Did a recession dampen people's travel plans?—and then moves to *strengthen* the organization's core value of customer service. The company's agents are directed to become more assertive in registering its customers in frequent-flier programs, or requesting special meals, or assisting with hotel or rental car reservations. While these services may not directly boost revenues, they will help consolidate the firm's client base. When the weather gets better, or the airlines lower their fares again, or the recession lifts, people will stick with the excellent service they've come to expect.

In the NFL there are teams that panic during the downturns, teams that hike without a compass. Every few years they coin new plans, new promises, new marketing slogans. They trade in philosophies like leased cars. They hire a coach with a new system, but they keep on the old regime's general manager and player personnel director. That's a potential problem right there—the coach can't coach the players he's given. When the team keeps losing, the new coach is fired. About every third coach, the front office is sent packing.

When management can't get on the same page, the book doesn't read too good.

Meanwhile, the owners are losing money, so they start to cut corners on the financial end. Or some new owners buy the team and give the coach an ultimatum: Win *now* or you're gone.

On occasion, teams like these put together some modest runs, but you don't see them in the Super Bowl. They've changed course more times than anyone can remember. They're frenetic about proving—to their shareholders, their fans, their media—that they're *doing* something.

And they never win anything big.

If you stacked these teams up against one of the perennial contenders, the talent gap might not be as great as you'd expect. It's the *philosophy* gap that separates them. The losers lack something vital: a sense of purpose.

For example: A company makes copper wire conduits with only high-grade metal, no matter what the cost of the raw material. Then a copper shortage hits, and the company faces a crossroads. Does it raise the price of its conduits, at the risk of losing market share? Does it resort to using lower-quality copper and hope that its customers won't notice the difference? Or does it maintain both its pricing and quality, and absorb a temporary dip in profit margin?

The company with integrity will be more likely to try that third option, even at the risk of lean times until the shortage is relieved.

IN AN UNSTABLE ENVIRONMENT, IT IS ESPECIALLY VITAL FOR LEADERS TO ARTICULATE THEIR VISION FOR THE ORGANIZATION—CLEARLY, EXPLICITLY, AND OFTEN.

When I came to New England two years ago, we had a junker of a football team. We were just trying to find tires to keep it out of the ditch, to get it on the road and running. But we also had a plan in place, a vision for where we were headed.

Whenever something went wrong that first season, people inside the organization would say: "We got to change this, we got to fix that." They had what I call the Texaco mentality. I kept reminding my staff that we couldn't just replace the carburetor, rotate the tires, give the defense an oil change, and assume it will be ready to go. That's what the fans want to do; that's what the press wants to do. When a team is losing, they'll clamor for change for the sake of change.

But when you're building something, you have to know what *you* want. You can't be unduly influenced by media scrutiny or public opinion. Assuming they're competent, leaders are in the best position to gauge how much progress they're making. They're the ones equipped with the road map.

EVERY ORGANIZATION, WHETHER IT'S FLOUN-DERING OR RULING THE ROOST, NEEDS A CALM, CLEAR VISION. ONLY PEOPLE INSIDE THE GROUP CAN CHART ITS COURSE; OUTSIDE VOICES MUST BE KEPT IN THEIR PLACE.

In 1990 my brother Don was part of a new management team that took the reins at First Fidelity Bank in New Jersey. At the time, the bank was in a tenuous position; it was in imminent risk of a takeover, either by the government or by some other group.

"This bank is on a death march," Don told me. "We're going to concentrate on three or four things here, and we're going to get these things done."

The new managers entered with a philosophy, and they were determined to put it in place, no matter how controversial or unpopular it might have seemed at the time. They consolidated operations and eliminated less productive departments. They installed a new computer system and made about thirty high-revenue acquisitions. Their battle isn't over yet, but the bank is on firmer ground, and its stock is up sharply. By keeping the faith, these leaders gave themselves the opportunity to prevail.

In 1983, my first year as a head coach in the NFL, my Giants team was stumbling toward a 3-12-1 record. I know for a fact that the front office was looking to replace me before the season ended; had one particular individual agreed to take the job, I would have been history. I might never have known whether I had what it took to compete at the highest level of my profession—I'd have been viewed as just another guy who wasn't good enough.

(Once they asked long-time NFL coach Chuck Knox if it wasn't true that bad calls by the officials tended to even out. "Yes, that's true," Knox replied, "provided you get to coach long enough to allow them to.")

My firing also would have set back the organization—not because I'm some irreplaceable genius, but because the Giants would then have had their fifth head coach in eight years. And each new one wants to bring in a new staff of assistant coaches, and a bunch of new leading players—the guys who can put *his* vision into play.

Over time, that revolving door will turn you into the New Orleans Saints, which suffered through twenty straight years without a winning season.

As the Giants decided whether to stick by me, the real challenge was in my court. That 1983 season marked the toughest year of my life. I lost both of my parents. My good friend and backfield coach, Bob Ledbetter, died suddenly from a stroke; Doug Kotar, the former Giants running back, lost a long battle with brain cancer. My team wasn't any good. My job—my dream job, with the team I'd rooted for as a boy growing up in Oradell, New Jersey—hung by a thread.

I named Scott Brunner our starting quarterback over Phil Simms. When Brunner struggled, I waffled and replaced him with Simms—who promptly broke his hand and was lost for the season.

As my father used to say, it's always darkest before it goes pitch-black. If I'd ever been tempted to jump ship on my own philosophy, that was the time.

IT'S EASY TO GET DIVERTED BY ALL THE VARIABLES OUTSIDE YOUR CONTROL, TO LET THEM EAT AWAY AT YOUR VISION AND SELF-CONFIDENCE. BUT DETOURS WILL DOOM YOU. LOSE FAITH IN YOURSELF, AND YOU'LL FULFILL YOUR OWN WORST PROPHECY.

Toward the end of the 1983 season, two conversations helped me turn the corner. The first was with Chuck Noll, the standout coach for the Pittsburgh Steelers. As I ticked off my woes, Noll listened patiently—and then he threw a whole new light on the situation.

"First thing, you better quit pouting around," he told me. "You've got to get *yourself* going first—if you don't do that, you've got no chance."

My second call was to Al Davis, the brains behind the Oakland Raiders and one of the men I've learned to trust most. "Quit worrying about the things you can't control," he said. "Just coach your team—that will determine whether you get to stay."

I was like the new restaurateur with a vision for an up-scale, family dining spot. Starting up a restaurant is tough, discouraging work; it's easy to get sidetracked by red tape and paperwork, unreliable or dishonest suppliers, unfriendly reviews in the local press. But the person in charge must stay true to his philosophy—by hiring the best available wait staff and line chefs, by rounding up the freshest ingredients—for that restaurant to survive its growing pains.

Back in 1983 I took my friends' advice to the bank. I cleared my head, put aside the distractions, and got on with the task at hand. By the time they told me I'd be back the next season, all my fear was gone. I said to myself, *I'm doing this my way now.* If I was going to fail, I wanted to have no one else to blame.

The following year the Giants made the playoffs. Two years after that, we won the Super Bowl. We succeeded because our organization, from top to bottom, had gathered the conviction to stay the course.

———

What is the Bill Parcells philosophy? It begins with the principle—drummed into me from my own playing days in high school—that aggressive, relentless defense is the key to any sport. In other words, you have to be able to stop people before you can be any good.

I believe that good coaching can cut down on penalties and turnovers, and that smarter, error-free teams have a better chance to win, even against more highly skilled opponents.

I think 100 yards of field position is worth 7 points, no matter how you get it—by running or passing the ball, by superior punting, or by having fewer penalties. (This obsession with field position—with *territory*—is a legacy of my assistant coaching days at West Point, where we'd get free advice from every major on the campus.)

My players don't argue with the officials, taunt opponents, or celebrate their own plays on the field.

I want a team that's in good physical condition, that plays to its strengths, that is mentally tough—that responds at the point in a game when winning or losing is determined.

As far as I'm concerned, these principles are nonnegotiable. They demand a hard line. If I tolerate players coming into training camp 25 pounds overweight, I can't effectively preach the importance of conditioning. In my first year at New England, an out-of-shape offensive lineman failed to make his time in our July shuttle run, which meant he couldn't pass our physical. He knew my rule; I'd warned the entire team about it months before. This guy had started every game the year before, but I cut him on the spot. I did the same last year with a veteran nose guard.

With out-of-shape rookies, who often have no clue, I have to be a little more tolerant. I segregate them into a special conditioning program until they can do their run. But by that time they're so far behind in practice that their chances of making the team are slim.

It isn't popular to draw hard lines these days, but I have no choice. To do less would undermine my credibility with the players—and our prospects of winning. My system isn't arbitrary. It comes out of my experience of what it takes to succeed in this business.

By way of analogy, consider a business which pays out a significant portion of its managers' remuneration in performance-linked bonuses. If you're a partner in that business, you're putting your money where your philosophy is; you're saying that hard and productive work will be rewarded. But once you monkey with that bonus structure, once you start playing favorites or reward yourself on a more lavish scale than others, your vision won't be worth much anymore. People will see through it to the real philosophy lurking underneath: that *who* you know at this company is more important than *what* you do.

TO ENLIST PEOPLE TO SHARE THEIR VISION, LEADERS MUST BE PREPARED TO WALK THE WALK.

Once a philosophy is fully accepted, it colors every aspect of the organization's life. It gives you a touchstone, a comfort zone, a buffer against adversity. When the '86 Giants went into halftime at the Super Bowl trailing Denver, 10–9, I didn't need to exhort them to win one for the Gipper. I simply appealed to our team's cornerstone principle: aggressive, disciplined, collective defense.

"You're lucky you're in it," I told my players. "Now go win it." We outscored Denver 30–10 in the second half.

Pro football is continually changing. Certain coaches and teams have put their signature on various fronts and formations. Most football fans have heard of the Houston veer . . . the flex . . . the West Coast offense . . . the wishbone . . . the monster defense.

When deployed effectively, all of these innovations have helped teams win. But newer isn't always better. In New York we did very well with a "lane" system derived from Bud Wilkinson's Oklahoma defense of the 1950s. If a principle is sound, there's no need to tart it up for the sake of originality. Football is an intricate game, but I like to keep our strategy as simple as we can.

Several years ago the Giants were manhandling the Jets in our annual pre-season game. By the fourth quarter the wolves are loose—we're playing the Jets to pass on every down. One of our linebackers sacks Ken O'Brien, the Jets' young quarterback. We call the same defense, and our guy knocks O'Brien down again; he gets rid of the ball, but just by a miracle.

Then all of a sudden my defensive coordinator, Bill Belichick, switches the defense so that our linebacker is no longer rushing. When I ask him what he's doing, Bill says, "I wanted to change up the coverage."

I'm astounded. I ask him, "Are you watching this game? We're getting ready to *kill* O'Brien."

Bill is one of the brightest men I know, but sometimes we get caught up in our own creativity and outsmart ourselves. If they can't hit your fastball, you throw it till you get twenty-seven outs, then you get to go home. If your architectural firm is hired to design an office building, you don't invest months in some fussy, elaborate, theme-park blueprint; you want something clean and functional, pleasing to the eye but also suited to the assignment.

WINNERS DON'T NEED TO BE RECOGNIZED AS BRILLIANT; THEY STRIVE TO BE DOMINANT.

Philosophies can't work as abstractions. They must be constructed, one part after the next—and in every business I can think of, the most important components are people.

Leaders must first know what people are needed to implement a system; then have the eye to identify them when they surface; then be able to integrate them into the organization; then teach and develop them so that they can function at their optimum; then direct them in actual day-to-day activity. Finally, once again, leaders must give the system time to succeed, while staying flexible enough to deviate from time to time.

Many systems collapse within the first two steps. If you

can't recognize the parts you need to build the structure you're after, your philosophy will falter out of the gate.

In football we find our components through draft picks, trades, and free agency. We're looking for certain prototypes. Our system works best with athletes who are bigger, stronger, and faster across the board. My goal is to become dominant at twenty-two positions; if we could do that, at least in theory, we'd win every game.

Al Davis was the one who imparted to me the need to have a definite philosophy—whatever it might be—on personnel. Davis hated the quick fix, the halfhearted improvisation, the easy compromise that corrodes the base of any organization. He held out for the players he wanted, and usually his insistence paid off.

In the real world, of course, you don't get everything you want, at least not right away. A coach has to mold the ingredients he has on hand, even as he looks for better ones. When I first came to the Patriots, I had to plug in several hold-the-fort guys just to make it through. I knew they wouldn't be with us long. Two years later, most of them are gone.

In some isolated cases you may even bend your specifications, as long as the exceptions are few enough to avoid capsizing your system. In New England I inherited a defensive back named Maurice Hurst who stood only 5-10, or about three inches short of my prototype for that position. But Hurst is fast and agile, with a nose for interceptions, and he has a chance to be the best cornerback I ever coached.

On the other extreme was a free agent we once signed for the Giants out of a small Baptist college. Like Hurst, he was a cornerback, but there the resemblance ended. This guy went 6-1, 203 pounds. He could run 40 yards in 4.5 seconds and he had great hands. He was one of the most skilled, graceful, athletic players I'd ever seen. At practice he'd be the star of the show.

But there was a reason the kid hadn't been drafted. I should have picked it up from the tape I watched of the Senior Bowl. The game was played in the rain—and our man was the only player whose uniform was clean. He just wasn't getting involved in the action.

As we entered our pre-season games, it became apparent that he would never make it in the NFL. He was missing something—confidence, ambition, the ability to rise to a challenge. He was what we call a "lure"—a guy who keeps you on the hook but never produces.

What many people in football—and in business—fail to understand is that there's a major difference between *skill* and *talent*. Skills are basic tools, and we all know they're important; in football, for instance, you can't play if you can't run. But skills alone can't carry you if you lack the talent to apply them in performance. And talent—and certainly *greatness*—is more than the sum of a person's skills. Larry Bird was a great basketball player, but not because he could run or jump or even shoot.

WITHOUT TOUGHNESS AND DEDICATION AND HEART, WITHOUT THE WILL TO PERSEVERE, ALL THE SKILL IN THE WORLD WON'T MAKE YOU A WINNER.

People refer to these qualities as "intangibles," but I disagree. Their presence—or absence—shows up in absolutely tangible ways. They directly affect the organization's bottom line, from won-loss records to quarterly earnings.

Consider the charming sales rep who has terrific communication skills, but is too lazy to make that extra call, or to hurdle a client's least resistance. I'd bet that his team would do better with a less polished but hungrier guy. In most cases it's easier to improve a person's presentation, to develop raw skills, than to instill a talent for hard work or resilience.

There's a football saying that sums it up: *If they don't bite when they're puppies, they usually don't bite.*

Which is why I put so much emphasis on interviewing my prospective draft choices or free-agent pickups. A half hour of candid conversation tells more about people than a mountain of statistics. For starters, I might ask them to name three or four of the most important things in their life. Family or religion often top the list, which is fine; football doesn't have to be number one. But football better be in there somewhere, or I'll deduce that this guy isn't all that interested in the job.

Sometimes I'll sting the player a little, just to see how he'll respond. Before we made Willie McGinest our first-round pick in 1994, I asked him whether we'd be getting "the Willie McGinest who played against Penn State, or the Willie McGinest who played against UCLA. I don't want the guy who played UCLA, because he isn't very good. But the guy who played Penn State has a chance to be great."

McGinest assured me that we'd be getting the Penn State version. More important, he didn't try to alibi or blame his college coach for his off day against UCLA. "I didn't play well," he admitted. "I got too emotionally involved, just couldn't cut loose."

What I'm watching for at these moments is *how* the player responds, not just what he says. If he cowers, or gets defensive, or seems overly shy or withdrawn, it's a warning flag. It's a sign he might have trouble with an abrasive, sarcastic, demanding coach—with someone like me.

I'm also curious about the person's family, his support system, his goals in life. Before I interviewed Reyna Thompson, a free agent who'd been left unprotected by Miami, I was already impressed by the videotape I'd seen of his work on punts and kickoffs. But I was sold when Thompson told me he was working toward a master's degree in business in the off-season. I knew then that we had someone special, a guy who was disciplined and well directed, who would fit into our team's philosophy. Thompson turned out to be the best special teams player I ever coached. He was a big-time contributor to our 1990 Super Bowl team, and even made the Pro Bowl.

When a player has the complete talent package, he's more likely to succeed at the next level, even when you're projecting him to fill a role that's new to him. At Clemson Andy Headen was bounced around to four different positions, from quarterback to strong safety to tight end. But I could see he had the size, speed, and skills to play outside linebacker, the primary point of attack in my defense. Headen's college coach assured me that he'd have no problem in the hitting department.

Drafted in the eighth round, Headen played linebacker for the Giants for seven years.

WHEN MATCHING PEOPLE TO ROLES IN THE ORGANIZATION, IT'S NOT ENOUGH TO WEIGH WHAT THEY'VE DONE IN THE PAST. TO GET THE RIGHT FIT, IT'S CRUCIAL TO CONSIDER WHAT THEY COULD *DO IF THE ENVIRONMENT ALLOWED THEM TO FLOURISH.*

Say you're chief of marketing, and you head up a task force on a newly developed product. As your team proceeds, you find that most of the good ideas are coming from a person who's been pigeonholed as an assistant in research. After the task force dissolves, you propose that the researcher be transferred to your department—or, at minimum, be included in the next interdepartmental project.

I've borrowed heavily from Al Davis in forming my philosophy on personnel. Like Davis, I'm always willing to take a chance for greatness—to bring in question-mark players with high-impact potential. One or two guys who wreak havoc— like Lawrence Taylor in New York, or Chris Slade here with New England—can keep your weaker people from being exploited; your competition has its hands full just fending off the pressure. Without those havoc guys, everyone on the unit has to perform to perfection, and that usually doesn't happen.

In the 1995 draft the Patriots got two third-round picks with first-round talent: cornerback Jimmy Hitchcock and running back Curtis Martin. Both of them slid because of past

injuries. Where other teams passed, we were comfortable making those choices. They fit in with our vision of a championship team, of how to become the best.

When you act with *integrity*, in accordance with your
organization's core principles, you're not taking a risk. You're
fulfilling your mission—and giving yourself the best possible
chance to succeed.

2.

FLEXIBILITY

SOME WISE PERSON ONCE SAID, "INFLEXIBILITY IS ONE OF THE worst human failings. You can learn to check impetuosity, overcome fear with confidence and laziness with discipline. But for rigidity of mind there is no antidote. It carries the seeds of its own destruction."

To succeed over the long haul, leaders must stay true to their vision, their core philosophy. But to flourish in a given situation, they must also be flexible in strategy and opportunistic in tactics.

That was my challenge with Lawrence Taylor, the greatest player I've ever coached—and the least predictable. Lawrence joined the Giants in 1981, the year I was hired by Ray Perkins as defensive coordinator. From his first day in camp, it was clear that Taylor was different. Aside from raw power and speed, he had brilliant instincts, relentless energy, and a knack for avoiding injury by contorting his body when in vulnerable positions. He was a football superman; he'd physically dominate the people who were playing him. Even when he messed up, he'd accelerate so quickly that he could recover and make the play.

In the sixth game of Taylor's career, against St. Louis, we call a defense in which the right outside linebacker drops back into pass coverage. Lawrence has a different idea; he decides to rush the quarterback. He sacks the quarterback, causes a fumble. We recover and eventually score a touchdown.

As he trots back to the sideline, I say, "Lawrence, did you know you were supposed to drop back in that defense?"

"Oh, yeah," he replies. From the start, this guy was highly coachable. He sincerely wanted to learn.

I tell him, "This situation is going to come up again—are you sure you have it?"

"Oh, yeah, Coach, I got it."

Sure enough, we call the same defense one quarter later. What does Lawrence do? He rushes. Not only does he sack the quarterback and force another fumble, but this time George Martin, our defensive captain, scoops the ball up and runs it in for a touchdown.

With the crowd in delirium, Lawrence comes back to the sideline. I just look at him, not saying a word—and then I see him slap himself in the head. "I did it again, didn't I?" he says.

"Yeah, you did," I tell him, doing my best to sound stern. "You know, Lawrence, we don't even *have* what you just did. It isn't in our play book."

"Well, Coach," he says, "we better put it in on Monday, because it's a dandy."

And put it in we did. Our defense now had a new wrinkle —thanks to Taylor's bold stroke and our willingness to use it.

———

My job was to integrate this special athlete within our system, to minimize the impact of his rookie mistakes, but at the same time to let Taylor *play*—to allow him to use his talent. To do that, I had to throw some standard practices and assumptions out the window. I've never been gung-ho about starting first-year players; they say that every rookie you start will wind up costing you a loss during the season, and I think they're right.

But Taylor couldn't wait. In his first pre-season scrimmage, he sacked the quarterback four times and recovered a fumble. In his first pre-season game, he made ten solo tackles, including two more sacks. He was decking quarterbacks with one hand, catching swift running backs from behind. It didn't take any genius for our staff to put Taylor in the lineup. He started every game that season, and helped lead the Giants to the playoffs for the first time in eighteen years.

TRADITIONS ARE MADE TO BE BROKEN. IF YOU'RE DOING SOMETHING JUST BECAUSE IT'S AL-WAYS BEEN DONE THAT WAY, YOU MAY BE MISSING AN OPPORTUNITY TO DO BETTER.

For example: A junior packaging designer is hired at a beverage company. Within months the newcomer is turning out better work than people with twenty years' experience at the job. While the company's traditional hierarchy may prohibit the designer from advancing too abruptly, it's clearly in management's interests to give the new employee more latitude and responsibility—and to follow up with raises and promotions in due time.

As Lawrence Taylor matured, we tried to tailor the Giants' internal environment to boost his success. In particular, we changed our pass defense design to take advantage of his ferocious rushing. In our old system, our right outside linebacker rushed the quarterback on about one of three pass plays, and fell back into coverage on the remainder. In our modified system, we let Taylor loose on *two* of three plays—and saw an exponential gain in wreaked havoc.

In turn, our opponents were forced to be flexible to keep our guy from overwhelming them. Against a conventional offensive formation, where Taylor played "against air," he could single-handedly disrupt the other team. Joe Gibbs admitted that his single-back, double-tight-end offense was designed to slow Taylor down by putting an extra blocker out there in front of him. By forcing the other side to adjust, our initial flexibility—tied to Taylor's basic superiority—gave us an edge, a leg up on winning.

A DOMINANT INDIVIDUAL CAN SOMETIMES CARRY THE DAY, BUT ONLY IF THE ORGANIZATION CREATIVELY OPENS DOORS FOR THAT TALENT TO FLOURISH.

Mature leaders accept the ingredients on hand. They tinker and experiment. If their system doesn't fit their personnel, they rethink the system. Down the road, they may seek out people who more closely conform to their vision. But in the meantime, they work with the available resources. They refuse to get discouraged or cynical about those who are less than ideal.

I've had position coaches who are never satisfied with the players we find them. Their glasses are always half-empty. This guy's too slow, they tell me. Then we bring in a faster guy, and he has bad hands, or poor balance, or lousy concentration. Or maybe he doesn't brush his teeth as much as they'd like.

At some point I'll decide to solve the problem in another way—I'll hire a new position coach, someone who's flexible enough to work with imperfect players.

Lawrence Taylor fit my physical prototype to a T; he was big, strong, fast, athletic. But football players aren't made from cookie cutters. Sometimes you turn up a David Meggett, who measures only 5-7, but whose speed and elusiveness makes him a dynamic receiver and return man. Or a Joe Morris, no taller than Meggett, who'd been nailed to the Giants' bench through his rookie season in 1982.

When I became head coach the following year, I was skeptical about Morris. I'd yet to see any evidence that he would be a very good player. I *knew* that he couldn't block or catch. On the other hand, Butch Woolfolk, our first-round draft choice in '82, wasn't coming close to my expectations. By 1984 I'd run out of options, and we put Morris in to see what he could do.

As it turned out, he could do plenty; he had good vision and straight-line speed. At nearly 200 pounds he was *strong*. Morris was tough and competitive, and over the last half of the '84 season he gained more than 500 yards. We put in things to compensate for his blocking, and we were set. Morris became our lead runner for the next four years, and set a franchise record for rushing in 1986.

IT'S EASY TO DOWNGRADE PEOPLE BY DWELL-ING ON THEIR WEAKNESSES. IT'S HARDER TO LOOK AT THEM WITH FRESH EYES AND IDENTIFY THEIR STRENGTHS—AND HOW THEY CAN HELP THE ORGANIZATION TO FUNCTION.

Consider the investment firm that has been stocked for generations with Ivy Leaguers, MBAs with pedigrees. Then a fresh bond salesman is hired out of the state university. He lacks polish; his suits don't always hang right, and you can hear his Brooklyn accent a mile away. But he also has incredible desire, an earnest manner that wins clients over, and a nose for an issue that's about to soar. He doesn't exactly fit in —he stands out, instead, and by his second year he ranks among the firm's top three earners.

Leaders tend to get labeled by their last big successes. In my case, I'm identified with my 1990 championship team in New York. I'm portrayed as a conservative, ball-control, clock-eating coach who wins with defense and special teams and power.

But people forget that just four years earlier, I'd coached a very different kind of team into the Super Bowl. On defense the 1986 Giants were more active and talented up front, smaller and less physical in the secondary. On offense we were athletic and explosive but not especially large. Our offensive line got the job done with "schemes": cross-blocking, trap-blocking, pulling at various angles.

That 1986 team went 14-2, then rolled in the playoffs to the largest cumulative margin of victory in NFL history. We demolished the Denver Broncos in the second half of the Super Bowl. But as good as that team was, we couldn't have replicated its success a few years later. We had to make significant changes—not just to replace aging players, but to cope with a changing environment.

For one thing, coaches like Buddy Ryan were transforming the way defense was played. In the old days you might see one or two defensive fronts, or deployments, on a given Sunday, and you'd rehearse your offense against those fronts. But now we faced more complex "multiple" defenses. You can only practice so long before players got bored, or exhausted, or injured, and there was no way we could prepare four different blocking schemes against four different fronts—that's *sixteen* repetitions on the same basic play.

At the same time, the athletes who manned those defensive fronts kept getting bigger and stronger and more dangerous. Their role model was our own Lawrence Taylor. We still had the original, but some of the copies out there were murder.

So we changed with the times. By 1990 our revamped offensive line relied on straight man-to-man power. Our strategy was simple: "We're going to make you guys play one-on-one football against us, and we'll see who's better."

Sixteen out of nineteen times, the scoreboard said the better team was the Giants.

But we didn't win simply because we had a bright new

strategy. We won because we'd collected the right prototypes for that *mano a mano* strategy to work. Jumbo Elliott, Bart Oates, Doug Riesenberg, Eric Moore—they all approached 300 pounds. They all were powerful, strong, smart, determined. And they blocked for a running back named Ottis Anderson, who was 7 inches taller and 30 pounds heavier than Joe Morris. With those horses in front of him, Anderson could run between the tackles all day—and sometimes it seemed that he did.

We still needed a flexible game plan; a coach is always adjusting to key variables like the score and time remaining. Still and all, I can't deny that the '90 Giants were less exciting than our earlier model. We passed only twenty-five times per outing, 15 percent less than in '86. If the game was in hand, we might stop passing altogether midway through the third quarter. It could be like watching paint dry. But no one could say we hadn't adapted to a new brand of football.

As change accelerates in the business world, only the adaptable will survive. A national brand company might be tops in its market for years with a powdered laundry detergent. But when the competition comes out with liquid concentrates, the top dog can't assume that its old flagship product will still dominate on its own—even though its powder is cheaper to use and more effective than the liquids. Brand loyalty buys you some time, but not eternity. So the company puts its research and development people to work to stay *ahead* of the trend—to come up with a liquid concentrate that removes stains better than the rest—and keep the pack at its heels.

Our flexibility on the Giants was challenged again in 1990 when Phil Simms sprained his foot two weeks from the end of the regular season. Phil was through for the year; our backup quarterback, Jeff Hostetler, would have to take us the rest of the way.

There were two ways to handle this unplanned transition. I could shoehorn Hostetler into the game plan we'd built around Simms, at minimal disruption to the rest of the team. Or I could alter the plan to play to Hostetler's strengths—to take the things he brought to the table and make him feel more comfortable in the job.

I chose the second course, the flexible course. Hostetler hadn't played enough to be as accurate a passer as Simms, but he was more mobile. He could elude the blitz and also throw on the run, which Simms couldn't do. With two weeks to go in the regular season, we had already clinched our divisional title. We had just one concern: how to get ready for the playoffs, when the chips would be on the table. So we used that time to put Hostetler's signature on the offense. We installed several bootleg passes and rollouts; we subtly tuned our design.

Even a veteran team needs time to absorb changes. Phil Simms had led the Giants, with few interruptions, since 1984. Now they had a new field general, and a revised set of marching orders. We struggled mightily on the road in those last two regular-season games; we beat Phoenix and New England, two doormats, by only 3 points apiece. We probably would have won with more ease with our old game plan.

But the new plan paid dividends in the playoffs. Late in the fourth quarter of our hammer-and-tong NFC championship game against San Francisco, Hostetler rolled out and hit Stephen Baker for 13 yards, which set up our game-winning field goal. And in our Super Bowl win over Buffalo, Hostetler had the best game of his career. After we fell behind by two scores, he engineered two long, poised, confident drives. He behaved as if this were indeed *his* team—which was our idea all along.

Now, flexibility has its limits. We'd assembled a cast of characters on the Giants with a definite profile. We weren't going to become a run-and-shoot team just because Jeff Hostetler was now the starter; you can't enter the Indy 500 with a Cadillac, no matter how well it runs.

In certain areas I am highly *in*flexible. If I fine one player fifty dollars a pound each day for being overweight in training camp, I'm not going to fine the next player twenty-five dollars. There's no latitude here. If you're late for a meeting, it will cost you two hundred bucks. You don't get a fifty-dollar rebate for a flat tire or some malfunction of your alarm clock. (On the other hand, if you were in a fifteen-car pileup and had to be extracted by the jaws of life, there might be some consideration.)

In my practice structure, my off-season training, the way I want my team to behave—these are all things I can control, and experience has shown that certain methods work best for me.

But even here there might be an exception. Great players are special, simply because they do more for the team than the rest. Their greatness may buy them preferential treatment in some areas. On the field, they may toss the book aside at times and play on instinct. They've earned the right to take chances

—to be *flexible*—because they've proved that their judgment is sound.

In 1990 I faced a dilemma with Mark Bavaro, one of my most courageous players. Bavaro was a remarkably self-motivated athlete. An unheralded fourth-round draft pick in 1985, he was voted All-NFL just one year later, when he had as good a season as any tight end ever.

Bavaro was a crushing blocker, the most sure-handed of receivers. He would go the extra mile and then some. But in 1990 he was also coming off major knee surgery. If I held him to the same practice standards as everyone else, he never would have made it to the playoffs.

So I made an exception. Throughout that season, Bavaro was restricted to light practice workouts during the week. He told me what he thought he could handle, and I always trusted him. His peers respected him so much that no one complained; they knew I was only letting him slide a little to benefit us all. And if anyone needled me about my double standard, I had a stock response: "You play like him, you can do it, too."

Bavaro missed only one game that season. He was our leading receiver in the playoffs, and had huge catches in our final scoring drives against both San Francisco and Buffalo. And it made absolutely no difference that he'd sat out some scrimmages that fall.

Every organization has their Mark Bavaro's from time to time, proven performers who are moving through a rough patch in life. There may be some personal turmoil—a divorce, a sick child or spouse, an alcohol problem being battled. The people in question may need time, patience, or special treatment, some special flexibility in working hours or project deadlines. In most of these cases, the flexible manager will reap a reward; after the storm has passed, the employees will be just as productive as before—and even more loyal to the company that supported them through their crisis.

CONSISTENCY IS OVERRATED. A LEADER IS OBLIGATED NOT TO BE CONSISTENT, BUT TO BE RIGHT—TO DO WHAT'S BEST FOR THE ORGANIZATION.

By the time I returned to coaching in 1993, after a two-year layoff, the environment had changed again. In today's game, teams have spread their offenses and opened up their attacks. The NFL is more pass-oriented, more flamboyant, more skill against skill, less power against power. Most teams are playing fast-break football; they want to get the ball in the open field to their best athletes, who then exploit one-on-one matchups. The quarterback's seven-step drop has been shaved to five steps, sometimes to three. Protections aren't as sound, so quarterbacks are forced to make quicker decisions—to get rid of that ball. Everything is happening faster than it used to.

The defense, meanwhile, has spread out to cover the offense. But every once in a while it condenses to rush more men than the remaining blockers can handle. Then it's up to the wide receivers to adjust, to shorten their patterns to two seconds or less, before the avalanche reaches their quarterback. It's the old cat-and-mouse game, revved up to warp speed.

My problem was that the New England Patriots had grown accustomed to playing the mouse. My personal leaning was that it was better to be the cat. But if we were going to grow some claws and sharp teeth, I knew I'd have to acclimate to a whole new way of operating.

I see the same thing happening in the business world. It's not that the old ways didn't work; they *had* to work at some point, or the company would have gone under. But as competition sharpens and technology advances, the old ways may not be enough anymore.

Not so long ago, anyone who made a long-distance phone call had to deal with Ma Bell; you either paid your bill to AT&T, or you bought a lot of postage stamps. But when the phone monopoly was broken, the old guard had to change. New rivals offered discounts and calling circles and cash incentives and frequent-flier miles. The Baby Bells didn't have to match MCI and Sprint, gimmick for gimmick, but there was no question they had to do *more*.

IF THE COMPETITION HAS LAPTOP COMPUTERS AND YOU'RE STILL USING YELLOW LEGAL PADS, IT WON'T MATTER HOW LONG AND HARD YOU WORK—THEY'RE GOING TO PASS YOU BY.

The Patriots team I inherited was nothing like either of my championship Giants teams. It was undersized on defense, error-prone, and inexperienced. That last was a drawback in the flexibility department. While veterans who've done their homework can help a coaching staff adjust during a game, younger players go by rote—they just do what the coach tells them.

New England also had an unusual talent in Drew Bledsoe, our young quarterback. Bledsoe is still a work in progress, but he has an arm that can do spectacular things. Some quarter-backs can't throw a corner pattern, or a deep comeback on the sideline, because the ball has to travel 40 yards on a line. Drew can throw anything you want him to. He opens up a whole new world in your passing design.

Our structure in New England is anything but conservative. To capitalize on Bledsoe's ability, we've spread our offense out on the perimeter. We are heavily pass-oriented—we threw 699 times last year, nearly twice as many as the 1990 Giants, and an all-time NFL record. (That was one record I'd never hoped to set.) With the signing of David Meggett, we're looking to use more skittery, open-field runners to whom Drew can dump the ball on first down. We're a long way from 3-yards-and-a-cloud-of-dust.

By and large, our offense is high efficiency, high production . . . and high risk. Do I like this new style? Not much, but I've had no choice. My job is to figure out what gives us the best chance to win *right now.* In my first two years with the Patriots, our defense was so weak that we *had* to score in bunches to be competitive. Now our defense is getting bigger and better. As it grows I'll gain more control over how we play. Our emphasis on smart, error-free football should begin to pay off.

I think the 1990 Giants could still win in today's NFL—they were that strong, that balanced, that talented. But I have no illusion of trying to re-create that team in New England. Bledsoe alone changes our course of development. Our ultimate goal is the same, but we'll be traveling a different path, adapting as we go.

A CLIMATE OF HIGH RISK-TAKING REQUIRES MORE FLEXIBILITY FROM THOSE SEEKING TO COMPETE. RIGIDITY ONLY MAKES AN ORGANIZA-TION LESS EFFECTIVE AND MORE PREDICTABLE TO ITS ADVERSARIES.

In the business world, IBM is the proof of the pudding— an example of just how damaging inflexibility can be. As Sally Helgesen pointed out in *The Web of Inclusion* (Currency/Dou-bleday), IBM was notorious for its bureaucracy and strict job definitions. Commands came down from the top, and filtered through an amazing number of layers till they reached the poor guy who actually had to do the work. The marketing executives ran the joint; the engineers were trained to connect the dots, to design products that the marketing wizards thought they could sell. It got to the point where IBM was mechanically defining what it thought the consumer needed, rather than responding to its customers.

In this atmosphere, with its rigid written guidelines for every procedure, there was little room for improvisation, or entrepreneurial spirit, or the bold stroke of individual genius. Well into the 1970s, as Apple established a new home market with its user-friendly, low-priced personal computer, IBM's leadership stood by its tried-and-true mainframes. The mar-keting division was dead against developing an IBM personal computer—they didn't know how to market it, so how could it succeed?

Finally, panicked at the loss of market share within its traditional business clientele, IBM swung into action, set up a special task force (by definition a flexible structure), and had its PC on the shelves within eighteen months.

Unfortunately for IBM, the old bureaucratic ways still prevailed. That might explain how the company came to be outflanked by its software partner, Microsoft, whose Windows program left IBM's homegrown OS/2 operating system in the dust.

Flexibility is a make-or-break component of motivation, the art of getting people to do what needs to be done. Your message, your tone, your timing—all of these vary with the circumstances and your target audience. The key is to find the right pitch to keep those ears open. I don't think you can fabricate emotion and be effective. But you can certainly modulate it for the occasion, and especially for the individual.

Jeff Hostetler, for example, was a very bright, very sensitive, very competitive guy. I would never yell at him—that would drive him into a shell, and away from the communication. If I thought he was missing something out there, I might say in an even tone, "Better watch out for this."

Phil Simms was more emotional. He could handle my temper, and return it in kind. If I felt exasperated, I might challenge him with: "You seein' the same game I'm seein'?" Or I might plead, "Would you just complete some passes here so I can sleep tonight?" Even when I raised my voice, I always made it clear I was on his side—he needed that support.

It's like running a print shop where your production guys are tough and reliable, but most of your salespeople are brittle, high-strung types. Where you might yell at the production side to get their attention, you'd be better off taking a salesperson aside, maybe into your office, for a quiet one-on-one meeting. Your objective is the same—to improve performance— but your style has to be flexible, or you'll demoralize your employees.

With Lawrence Taylor I could pull out the stops. He was cocky and self-assured, and held any sign of weakness in contempt. So I'd march right up to him and say, "Lawrence, if you don't knock this quarterback down four times today, we have no chance." It's easy to coach the great competitors; they rise to any challenge.

When the Giants played Washington at home in 1989, Joe Gibbs decided that Taylor was not going to beat them that day. The Redskins double-teamed him on every play with a tackle and tight end, and occasionally they sent a running back to *triple*-team him. Taylor was neutralized; he had about one tackle. But the rest of our defense did very well—they were playing ten against eight, after all—and we won a close game.

Sportswriters don't keep their jobs these days by just telling you who won or lost. At my post-game press conference, the big question was: "What's the matter with Taylor?"

The next week we play the San Diego Chargers, coached by Dan Henning, who'd worked a long time with Gibbs. He sees the tape of the Washington game and decides to try a similar strategy. Once again, it's quite effective, to Taylor's frustration; once again, we win a tight game.

And once again the press demands: "What's the matter with Taylor?"

So the following week in practice, I say, "You know, Lawrence, I'm going to change your first name from Lawrence to 'What's-A-Matter-With?' Because the only time anyone mentions the name Taylor, that's how they preface it.''

At first he laughs, but as the week goes on, I could tell it's bugging him.

"Hey, What's-A-Matter, you're supposed to go inside on this play.''

"Look, What's-A-Matter, you got to nail this guy.''

Our next game is Monday night, at home against Minnesota. The Vikings are riding high; most of the experts have them headed to the Super Bowl. We lose Simms with an ankle injury on our first possession, and trail by a touchdown at halftime.

But Lawrence is magnificent. He gets eleven tackles and two and a half sacks, forces two fumbles and keeps one of them. He's on a rampage; he's all over the field. After we win the game, 24–14, I walk off through the exit tunnel. Just as I turn right toward our dressing room, this *thing* jumps on my back and clamps over me. I don't know who it is, but I know he's very strong.

Then Taylor puts his head right up to my ear and says, "I'll tell you what, Coach, they ain't gonna ask you what's-a-matter tonight!''

When you come up against a force of nature like Lawrence Taylor, you've got to give some ground or the relationship will rupture. Flexible leaders understand how to bend to reality without bruising their pride or compromising their philosophy. They know that there's only one unbreakable rule: Locate the best path that presents itself at the time, then move ahead without looking back.

3.

LOYALTY

THREE THINGS CAN RUIN ANY ORGANIZATION.

One is your competition. If your product line can't compete, you're in big trouble—whether your rivals are Toyota and Honda or the Dallas Cowboys and the Washington Redskins.

The second is public perception, as shaped by the media. If you're always seen in a negative light, your group's morale will likely go under—along with your performance.

The third factor? Division from within—*and this is the greatest threat, hands down.* When your team is united, it can ward off any flak from negative perceptions; it won't make any difference what outsiders think. And when your team is working together, your competition will have fewer weaknesses to exploit.

But a team divided against itself can break down at any moment. The least bit of pressure or adversity will crack it apart.

THE FIRST TASK OF LEADERSHIP IS TO PRO-MOTE—AND ENFORCE—COLLECTIVE LOYALTY, ALSO KNOWN AS TEAMWORK.

Everyone thinks they know what teamwork means, but very few people really understand it. To begin with, you need to ask: What kind of team do we want? A recent article in the *Wall Street Journal* defined organizational models in terms of various sports. Some companies are run like baseball teams, where each person's role is rigid and distinct. The shortstop doesn't switch with the first baseman; the center fielder doesn't run in to catch. Until the ball is thrown, only one fielder is in motion: the pitcher. Until the batter hits the ball, it's a one-on-one game. Then other players react to the outcome of that pitcher-batter confrontation.

Baseball-type organizations can divide themselves very, very easily. They tend to foster the equivalent of the hulking first baseman who hits thirty home runs and figures he's a star. The slugger doesn't care that he struck out a hundred fifty times, or that he couldn't move a runner over when the game was tight, or that he fielded his position like a sumo wrestler in snowshoes.

Worst of all, the slugger doesn't care that his team finished fifth, thirty games out. "It's not my fault," he'll tell you. "I'm doing *my* job."

Football-type organizations are different. While roles are still well defined—runners run, throwers throw, kickers kick—everyone must work in synchronization for the team to click. In executing a play, eleven moving parts need to be strictly coordinated. To make it even more challenging, smaller groups are interwoven within the larger unit. A tight end meshes his blocking with an offensive tackle; the fullback blocks for the halfback.

And way out in the field, like the sales rep in a remote branch office, is the split end—who has to know what the quarterback is going to do, even if he couldn't hear what was said in the huddle against the noise of the crowd.

Taking this point a step further, the offense can't work in isolation from the rest of the team. Its field position—which helps determine what plays can be called—is created by the work of two *other* units: the defense and special teams.

Disunity will kill you quick in this kind of organization. One maverick can capsize the ship. Think of a symphony orchestra about to get its cue from the conductor. If the tuba comes in before the violins, it's not going to sound too good.

In my line of work, teamwork is all-important. Every player, from the starting quarterback to the special teams rookie, is interdependent. We have this sign up in our locker room: *"Individuals play the game, but teams win championships."*

You could place the same sign inside any company in this country. Winning managers keep track of office politics, and for the disunity that lurks there. They stay alert to signs of backstabbing or jealousy. It can be tempting to ignore these things, to push aside the gossip and get on with your job— except for the fact that this *is* your job. No rumor is petty if it reflects an employee's discontent. And when people are worried about their place in the organization, working together takes a back seat to watching one's back. You need to deal with these issues as though they were intruders in your home;

you need to challenge them up front and send them on their way.

We were lucky in New York. Our top players—Lawrence Taylor, Phil Simms, Mark Bavaro, Carl Banks, Harry Carson—were all team-first. The only thing they were "selfish" about was winning. When your great players are team players, everybody else falls in line.

When your top player is Derrick Coleman, you've got no shot.

The best thing about Lawrence Taylor was that he understood that he was just a cog in the wheel. The awards he earned—rookie of the year, defensive player of the year, MVP—never swallowed him. No matter how much adulation he got from the fans and the media, he only cared about three things:

Did the team win?

Did he contribute to that win?

Who were we playing next?

Lawrence would inspire other players almost every week—not just with his amazing athletic talent, but with his team-first commitment. Once he ran across the field to nail a ball-carrier . . . after tearing a hamstring midway into the play.

Phil Simms, meanwhile, was the ideal field general. He could rally the troops and assume tremendous responsibility without pulling rank. When pass protection broke down and he got clobbered, he'd rarely complain, never berate an individual lineman. Once in a while he might try to wake up the whole line—"It's like a jailbreak back here!"—but it was always in a manner that reminded the others that he was on their side.

I've always taken time with my quarterbacks to explain what their job was: to get their team into the end zone, to score touchdowns. The other statistics don't matter much to me. If you complete 30 percent of your passes but the team scores four touchdowns, you've done your job and I'm going to be pleased.

Simms understood this from the start. As Joe Morris developed, Phil didn't merely accept the Giants' shift to a more run-dominated offense; he embraced it. He knew it would make his job easier, and the team more successful.

Unity is a corny concept in this age of instant heroes. The popular wisdom tells the coach, "You're restricting these players if you don't let them express themselves, if you don't take full advantage of their individual talents." They want Drew Bledsoe to throw the ball every down. Why don't we do that? Simply because it's not the best way to win.

Which reminds me of one of the two or three most ludicrous things I've heard in the last ten years—that Dean Smith was "the only guy who could hold Michael Jordan under 20 points."

That comment equates scoring with winning basketball. In fact, what Michael Jordan learned at North Carolina went far beyond scoring. He learned how to guard people, how to pass the ball. He learned how to become effective *within a team system*, and he carried that trait to the Chicago Bulls. The Bulls won their first championship not when Jordan averaged the most shots or points, but when the *team* developed to where he could exploit his full range of skills—by passing to Scottie Pippen on the wing, for one thing.

It's easy to spot team-first players. They're the ones who are determined to win every time, who are willing to do whatever it takes—and not just once in a while. Joe Montana was like that. Charles Barkley is like that. Every time you see Barkley straining for a rebound, you can tell that he wants to win. He *hungers* to win. And he's never shy about reminding less gifted teammates that he can't win without them.

Barkley can sing solo, but he knows that he needs the choir.

If you're the top-performing rainmaker in a big accounting firm, it's not enough to bring in your parade of clients and bask in your own glow. To serve the company best, you also need to share your techniques with colleagues, and refer your spare leads to them—even if it means you might stand out a little less. And you need to *listen* to those colleagues, too; you might find to your surprise that they can teach you something.

WHEN SELFISHNESS IS TOLERATED, THE EN-TIRE ORGANIZATION IS IN JEOPARDY. WHEN LEADERS STOP TRIMMING DEAD WOOD, THE WHOLE TREE SOON FALLS.

In 1988 the New York Giants were just two years removed from a championship. We had a veteran team that was starting to get old in several key positions. It was like Custer's last stand—the players still had enough competitive spark to win some games, but collectively they couldn't get beyond that, to the next step. It wasn't our talent; it was our team's mentality. They weren't quite as hungry as before. They weren't willing to pay the price to stay at the highest level. And, sad to say, they weren't as unified.

Ever since that first Super Bowl, a few of our players had gone sour. These weren't our biggest stars, the ones with a chance to go to Disney World if they win the Super Bowl. They were second-tier players, prominent starters who'd grown jealous of the ones at the top. They were vying for book contracts, TV commercials, endorsements—all the fruits of the limelight. They were mouthing off at practice to their position coaches. They figured they'd been driving the bus; in fact, they'd just been sitting near the front.

These guys had always seemed to be team-first players, but now they showed their true colors. When it came time to distribute the credit, they were me-first all the way.

Even worse, these veterans were now a negative influence on our younger, up-and-coming players—the ones who should have been willing to run through any wall for the team. Here was our nucleus for the future, and they were starting to show the first signs of arrogance and smugness. They had these little attitudes. And *they* hadn't achieved anything yet.

We were breeding a culture of mediocrity. We were like the radio station staff that wins the local ratings war for the first time, and then trips over itself in clambering for perks and rewards. The afternoon deejay is sure *he's* the one who got them to the top spot. So is the ad manager, the morning drive-time producer, and the guy who built the radio tower. They're not working together anymore; they're competing for recognition. And if any of them think they're not getting what they deserve, that station isn't going to be such a happy, successful family for long.

Or take the ad exec who's eager to share the load of developing a new campaign with a copywriter and art director, but grabs for all the credit when he presents the team's ideas to the client.

Had our Giants veterans grown selfish? I think so. A selfish outlook will translate into a loss of team resolve—a reluctance to do what you know the team needs to be successful. An unwillingness to make the essential sacrifices.

In football this shows up in subtle ways. Say our split end isn't the primary receiver on a play, so he doesn't run his route out full speed. Result: He fails to draw the attention of an opposing safety, who breaks up a pass to our flanker. Or say we're running to the right, and our left tackle is nonchalant about cutting off the defensive end on the backside of the play; he assumes he's not a factor. Result: The defensive end runs our back down and cuts our potential gain from 8 yards to 2.

If you don't want to hit 'em anymore, it's time to step away from the ring. At some point, sooner or later, we all get weary of the fray. It happens to every player, every coach, every executive, every sales rep. It's going to happen to me—I know that day is coming, and it's probably coming soon. It isn't anyone's fault; there's no shame in it.

But a lot of guys in business retire and announce it three years later. They've stopped striving to perform; they just haven't gotten the gold watch yet. These people can get by on guile, but they'll only take the company so far.

We wound up 10-6 in 1988, and we knew it was time to

make big changes. Over the next two years we replaced about fifteen players, a third of the team. Among them were two of those second-tier guys—the wannabe bus drivers. Had we stuck with the same group, we would have gone 8-8 or 7-9 in 1989; with our new team, we moved back up to 12-4. And had we not made those changes, we probably would have slid to 5-11 by 1990. Instead, we won our second Super Bowl.

It was tough to send some of these players away. In their prime they'd given us everything they had—they'd gone to war for us. I'd remember them hobbling onto the plane after a road game, carrying their own IV lines to stop the cramping. I felt tremendous loyalty to those individuals. But my greater loyalty was to the team.

When I got to New England in 1993, the situation was even more urgent. Over the last three seasons the Patriots had won a *total* of nine games. I knew better than to think that I could wave my magic wand over the same collection of people and transform their losing mind-set. I knew we needed more team-first players.

In any organization, the tone is set by the leaders, both within management and among the troops. So I took a hard look at New England's incumbent quarterback, a nice young man named Hugh Millen, and I knew we had a problem. Millen had led the Patriots to a 6-10 record in 1991—a five-game improvement over the year before—and he'd convinced some people, including the local media, that he might be capable of bringing the team back into contention.

But I had my doubts. I'd watched New England closely that year, and I'd seen Millen make critical judgment errors that kept his team from winning three more games. When the Patriots slid back to 2-14 in 1992, I wasn't surprised.

The clincher came that next spring, when we started an off-season program for our quarterbacks. Scott Zolak, the young backup, jumped right into it. But Millen was rehabbing some minor injury and continued to work on his own schedule. He seemed to be expecting preferential treatment—and from where I sat, he'd done nothing to deserve it. He was lazy. He wasn't prepared to make sacrifices. When he came into my office to discuss his status, I listened patiently and thought to myself: *There's no way this guy's going to be my quarterback.*

Two months later we drafted Drew Bledsoe and Millen was gone.

He wasn't the only one. By the fall of 1994 we'd cleared out eighteen of the "old" Patriots, and I was the guy who had to tell them they were through here. When you rise to a leadership position and seek to invigorate a business, any business, a part of your job—probably the toughest part—will be to let people go. You can't ever disrupt a person's life lightly; before making a change, you need to give that individual every chance to get with the new program.

At some point, however, you've got to ensure a collective loyalty to the company's goals. The rugged individualists, the ones who set their own agendas, are often powerful personalities who've developed a certain camp following. But they can also poison the atmosphere within your organization, and a responsible leader cuts them loose.

As soon as we made it through that period in New England, I could feel the difference. Though our new team was still maturing, we knew we were in it together—we were all trying to win.

But a leader can't ever take teamwork for granted. Selfishness is all around us in this society, and you have to stay vigilant to keep it out of your organization. We have a young linebacker here named Todd Collins, a good athlete who got his first start in the fifth game of the 1993 season. That happened to be in Phoenix, where you can have 95-degree weather into October.

Collins is also a key special teams player, and he's worried about getting too tired to function. He wants to stay fresh to perform at his best on defense and solidify his position. So what does he do? He begs off some of his assignments with the special teams coach, who accommodates him.

I don't find out about this until after the game. On Monday, when the team watches the game tapes, I say lightly, "Collins, let me ask you a question—are you a coach or a player?"

"I'm a player," he says.

I follow it up: "Do players get to say who plays what in a game, or do the coaches decide?"

Now he's sweating: "The coaches do that."

"But it's my understanding," I say, "that on Sunday you were telling the coaches where you wanted to play, and what you wanted to play, and when you wanted to play. You want the whistle, Collins? You can take this whole operation over, if you want it."

"No, I don't want it," says Collins, who's looking for the nearest hole.

"That's good," I say. "The next time you're worried about fatigue, ask the defensive coordinator to take you off the defense—because I need good special teams players."

WHEN TEAM-FIRST PEOPLE ARE FORCED TO CHOOSE FROM AMONG TASKS OR RESPONSIBILITIES, THEY PICK THE ONE MOST VALUABLE TO THE ORGANIZATION—NOT THE ONE THAT BEST PROMOTES THE INDIVIDUAL.

These choices must be made all the time, and the people involved don't always have freedom to do the choosing. Say your company has embarked on a crucial marketing project, and you've hit a snag. A leading sales rep is called in to shore up the team, even though it will mean a personal sacrifice of numbers and commissions. A smart boss will acknowledge the sacrifice and chip in a bonus to compensate, while affirming the sales rep's value to the organization.

Vincent Brisby is another up-and-coming youngster on our team, a kid from Louisiana. He's my starting split end, and I like him very much—in fact, he's on his way to becoming a coach's pet. In his rookie season he catches a couple passes . . . and suddenly I see him out there signaling first downs, acting flamboyant, doing things that *nobody* on my team has ever done.

I just take his ass out of the game, and I tell him, "I don't want tin soldiers here, but I want a *team*. If your teammate makes a good play and you want to go over and jump on top of him, go do it. Any exuberance you show for your teammates is acceptable. But any of this *me* stuff—this beating your chest, taking your helmet off, and mugging to the crowd— that's not acceptable. If you want to do that, go play somewhere else."

Brisby got the message. Now *he's* the one who tells the incoming rookies, "Some things don't go around here—I found out the hard way."

The most common form of disloyalty is the behind-the-back complaint. Bitching is our national pastime. Walk into any business, and 75 percent of the things you'll hear will be negative. Effective leaders need to keep a close eye on their organization's hostility index. The best way to lower the index is by confronting the source. Right away. To his face. And in front of the whole group, if possible.

In my line of work, a running back might complain that the coach never calls his number. Or a wide receiver might gripe that the quarterback won't throw him the ball.

When I get wind of this, I don't appeal to team loyalty; the team is not a high priority for these people at the moment. I act as a reality check, to put out more accurate public information. "I don't know why the hell you're complaining about not getting the ball thrown to you," I'll begin. "Two times he did throw to you, you were covered, and the third time you dropped the ball in a clutch situation. If you just do your job to get open and quit worrying whether the ball's coming your way or not, the ball will start coming back to you. Because the quarterback is going to throw it to the guys who are open."

*WHEN THERE IS GRUMBLING IN THE RANKS,
SHIFT THE RESPONSIBILITY BACK ON TO THE
COMPLAINERS. GET THEM TO THINK ABOUT HOW
THEY CAN HELP THE ORGANIZATION, RATHER
THAN THE OTHER WAY AROUND.*

There's a dispute inside your insurance company, which does a high volume of new transactions. The claims adjusters are griping that the agents are so eager to make sales that they're writing policies too loosely. The upshot: a wave of frivolous claims. The agents, meanwhile, claim that the adjusters are rejecting legitimate claims, which hurts the agents' reputation and policy renewal rate.

As office manager, it's your job to sit both sides down together and work out some guidelines and policy language that are agreeable to all, including your attorneys. The compromise may not be perfect, but the benefit to morale should lead in a straight line to higher productivity and revenue.

I'm a big believer in what we call unit pride. We want our receivers or our linebackers to pull for one another; if they can sustain that spirit within the smaller group, they'll normally extend it to the larger team. Every football fan remembers the "Steel Curtain" and the "No-Name Defense"; the names gave those units a prideful identity, and that's a healthy thing.

At the same time, I know that football teams typically divide between the offense and the defense. If the offense is struggling, you'll often hear: "How many times do we got to stop them before you guys score?"

A leader has to stomp that kind of thinking like grapes. My main point, and I make it over and over again, is that *we win or lose as a team*, as a group of forty-five players and eleven coaches. That's from day one, that's in concrete. If the offense scores 48 points and we lose 49–48, they didn't score enough. If the defense holds our opponent to 18 points and we lose 18–17, they gave up too many.

Team spirit doesn't fall from the sky. It needs to be fed by daily interactions and shared experience. After the 1983 season, when twenty-five Giants players went on the injured reserve list, I hired a strength coach, Johnny Parker, and asked the owners to pay for a weight room. The new facility did more than reduce our injuries and help get us ready for the next season. It became a team clubhouse, where players and coaches could meet informally and get to know each other better. It strengthened our unity; it was a key ingredient in the success we'd have in the years that followed.

I constantly look for ways to bring our team together. When we gather to watch the game tapes on Monday, we don't split into units at the start. For forty-five minutes we all watch the special teams tape. It's a chance for the backups to get their share of peer recognition. Before the salary cap made them illegal, I used to award small cash incentives to the top special teams performer of the week. The money was secondary; the point was to applaud essential contributions to the team.

Any business can do the same. You might choose, for example, to recognize a top secretary each month with complimentary theater tickets or dinner for two. While lower-profile, lower-paid employees may especially appreciate these incentives, you'll find that company stars gear up for them as well.

We all value public recognition; we all like to win the contest; we all like to take home the prize. As the old saying goes, found money spends a lot better than earned money.

FOR THE TEAM-FIRST MIND-SET TO TAKE ROOT, IT MUST BE REINFORCED AT EVERY OPPORTUNITY.

Like most organizations, football teams contain all sorts of people and personalities, a broad range of ethnic and sociological backgrounds. The leader has to take all these people and unite them. You can't do it unless everyone understands the common denominator—the shared purpose that brought them to the game in the first place, before the agents and big contracts and endorsements came their way.

As I tell my players, "This game can make you wealthy; it can make you famous. It can give you a lot of things, but it can't give you a championship. You've got to earn that. And unless you're willing to pay the collective price—to play as a *team*—you will not get it. Because the competition is too great, and someone else will have that little edge."

The same absolute necessity of showing one's loyalty applies to management as well. You can't expect the people in the trenches to give their all to the organization if the top honchos in the home office care only for *their* perks and position. People tolerate a lot of quirks in their boss, but they've got to know they'll be defended when they come under unfair attack.

Loyalty has to flow both ways, up and down; if you're not getting any, you'll soon have none to give back.

When I worked for the Giants, general manager George Young and I were never the closest of friends. But we knew we had to work together, and our philosophy in building a team was pretty much the same. There were times when Young's conservatism drove me crazy. Yet looking back at it, he served to balance a somewhat impulsive young coach. We both knew we needed one another to succeed.

Of the many qualities we demand of our own staff, loyalty heads the list. I have no problem with ambitious assistant coaches; I was once one of them myself. I felt proud when two staff members from our 1990 Giants championship team, Bill Belichick and Tom Coughlin, left for bigger opportunities elsewhere. Both of them are creative, strong-minded, assertive, dedicated leaders. But when they worked with me in New York, they also understood who was in charge. They were willing deckhands; they weren't pushing to steer the ship.

Belichick, now going strong as head coach for the Cleveland Browns, had as much to do as anyone with our success in New York. When I first came to the Giants in 1981, as defensive coordinator, Belichick was coaching special teams. On his own initiative, he spent every spare moment in practice assisting me with the defense. Soon he was my right-hand man. He didn't get paid extra for this work; he wasn't awarded some fancy title. He just learned and contributed as much as he could, and he carved out a larger role in the process. When I became head coach, it was obvious that Belichick would be my defensive coordinator; he was already doing the work.

By doing more for the organization, he wound up helping himself.

There are assistant coaches in this league who promote themselves at their team's expense. They squabble over credit for some component of the game plan; they behave as if their unit wore a different-colored uniform. I've seen offensive coordinators work overtime to ingratiate themselves with the media. They are quick to cite *their* glowing statistics—and to blame last Sunday's loss on the defense. More than a few of these guys have parlayed a media-built reputation into a head coaching job.

They usually don't last too long; a me-first coach is hard-put to field a unified team.

I welcome opinions, ideas, even disagreements from my coaching staff. But once I set the course, we all get behind it. And to preempt division from within, we have one simple, undemocratic rule: There's just one public voice for the New England Patriots. The rule does wonders in reducing controversy. Since I'm the only coach who speaks to the media, my staff never has conflicts in print.

One team, one voice—it seems logical to me.

When a product line fails to carry its weight, an alert company will divert its resources to a line performing better. Some people may be transferred or laid off. Sometimes an entire department may be eliminated. In any case, the status quo will be disrupted. But management has no choice if they want to stay competitive.

It's the same in my business. A lot of rookies in the NFL are hurt by tunnel vision. The first thing they do is size up their chances to survive the cut. A young wide receiver assumes that the coach will keep six players at his position—and that as long as he clings to the sixth rung in the pecking order, his job will be safe.

What that rookie doesn't understand is that he's *also* competing with the sixth running back and the third tight end and the eighth linebacker and the ninth offensive lineman. We can't fit all of these marginal guys onto a fifty-three-man roster, and nothing is in stone. If we come up with an outstanding group of defensive backs, people who will strengthen our special teams, we might go with only four or five wide receivers that season.

That number-six guy is out on the street. He just didn't *do* enough to impress me.

This process can also work in the opposite, more positive direction. There might be budget lines for three programmers on a systems staff, and all three incumbents are solid performers. A junior programmer is hired at a lower salary slot, with no clear path to advancement. But if the new hire shows enough talent and initiative, if the person proves too good to risk losing to a rival firm, a smart manager will find a way to fiddle with the budget and promote the up-and-comer.

A PERSON'S VALUE WILL BE WEIGHED ON WHAT HE CONTRIBUTES TO THE ENTIRE ORGANIZATION, NOT BY THE TRADITIONAL NICHE HE FILLS IN A GIVEN DEPARTMENT.

We can't always choose the roles we play within our organization. Often careers are stalled by factors outside a person's control. Maybe the company has stopped growing, making promotions harder to come by. Or maybe the person is in the wrong spot at the wrong time. When I coached at Florida State University, I recruited a player named Waldo Williams, who was also an excellent baseball catcher. Waldo opted to sign with the Cincinnati Reds—who coincidentally had a guy named Johnny Bench.

Three years later, going nowhere, Waldo was back trying to play football.

Andy Headen was one of the best athletes on my Giants teams. He went 6-5 and 242 pounds, with outstanding speed. He could have started on most teams in the league. But Headen's position was right outside linebacker, and he wasn't going to beat out our incumbent, Lawrence Taylor. So we tried to carve out a role for him as our "nickel" backer in passing situations, as a mainstay of our special teams. For seven years Headen contributed to the depth that made the Giants so tough to beat.

It's a real test to accept a lesser role, to subordinate your ego for the good of the organization and for your own survival. At some point you may decide to try your luck with a different company—to become a free agent, in our business. But often you're better off staying put. And staying ready, just in case opportunity knocks.

For many successful companies nowadays, "streamlining" often translates into slower advancement. If you're going to further your career, you can't just do your job well and assume that promotions will come at conventional intervals.

Nor can you keep jumping to greener pastures, where you're likely to face similar obstacles—and have less seniority to protect you if your new employer decides to downsize. The solution is to do *more*—to get beyond your job description, to expand your skill package and your role within the organization, even though you're operating under the same old title and pay scale.

In my first year with New England, we signed a running back named Corey Croom, a nondescript free agent from Ball State. I didn't even know who he was when he first showed up; I certainly had no particular expectations. But as training camp progressed, I started to notice him. Croom is just an average athlete, a plugger, but he had staying power. He was a little bit tougher than the next guy. He never got hurt, and he was always prepared. We can *depend* on Corey Croom—he's one of the Jeeps that we need to back up our Porsches.

When we made the playoffs in 1994, we started Croom against Cleveland, and I wasn't surprised when he did a solid job. He might never be a star, but he should last in this league for eight or nine years.

With other players, ego wins out. Lionel Manuel joined the Giants in 1984, and started at wide receiver for our 1986 Super Bowl team. By 1988 he'd become a little too comfortable. By then we had a young, hungry kid named Mark Ingram just coming into his own. By 1990 Ingram was a superior weapon to Manuel, and he took away his starting job.

Manuel couldn't adapt to his new role. He started showing up late for practice, dozing through meetings. He could have kept his job and his salary, but his spirit was broken. Manuel just wasn't dependable anymore; he wasn't the same guy. By the eleventh game of the season we had to let him go. I didn't enjoy doing it, but I had no choice. "I didn't cut this guy," I told his agent. "He got fired, but he fired himself."

That move startled the other players. But it also made clear that *no one* would be allowed to interfere with our quest for another championship. No one was bigger than the team.

There are two conflicting mentalities in any organization: *to have* and *to be*.

People with a *to have* mentality are obsessed with what they can *get* out of their jobs: a bigger salary, and all that it can buy; promotions and status; recognition and fame.

People with a *to be* mentality concentrate on what they can *give* to the organization: their best efforts to help the team succeed.

The *to have* mentality is a dead end. It can never be a sufficient motivator to win at the highest level. I've seen it time and again: A player plays for his next contract, but once he gets it he's no longer the same player. He's reached his goal, but his goal was too small. Complacency sets in.

As I once told Leonard Marshall, a terrific player on my Giants teams who was looking to negotiate a new deal: "If you play to be the best you can be, the next contract will come."

Phil Simms was a *to be* guy from the start. He didn't come into the league with some rubber-stamped credential; he was just a guy out of Moorhead State. He never stopped working to improve himself, to help his team win.

Ben Coates came to the Patriots out of someplace in

North Carolina called Livingston College. Through tremendous dedication he's become one of the most productive tight ends in the league—and earned a handsome new contract as a result.

Picture two equally productive salesmen. One of them keeps nagging his boss for a bigger corner office. The other one prods the boss for advice on how to expand his customer base, and follows that advice with good results. When a bigger office opens up, you know the second salesman will get it. He has so much business now that he *needs* it more than his colleague.

There was no room for *to have* guys when I entered the coaching profession—there just wasn't much out there to have. Coaching was like teaching; you had a nice, modest life, and maybe at the end you became an athletic director. The biggest names in the profession—Vince Lombardi, Red Holzman, Casey Stengel—were older men who eventually went off into the sunset. There weren't any millionaire coaches.

I just wanted to be the best coach I could, at the highest level. For the first twenty years of my career, my wife and I did well to pay our bills. But I was happy, and satisfied; I was doing what I wanted to do.

Nowadays it's different. Players enter the league thinking that it's just a business—that it's all about money.

I detest that mentality, because it's *not* about money. It's about achievement, and winning, and championships. It's about proving that you can do something better than the other guy.

And it's about helping a team do more than individuals ever could.

———

In my view, a head coach is the one person consistently trying to pull his team together. Everyone else is pulling it apart. That goes for the media, the owners, the agents, the players' relatives—even the players themselves.

I'm not saying they do this on purpose. But they all have private agendas. An owner wants to impress his friends, so he brings them around to disrupt a practice. Reporters are searching for a scoop; if they sow disunity in the process, so be it. The agents are hunting bigger contracts—and the road to big bucks is paved with *individual* statistics. The players' wives and brothers always think their guy should have more playing time, more notoriety, more money.

Even the equipment manager has ulterior motives. If it's raining outside, he'll suggest that the team work indoors. The head coach knows his players need bad-weather practice, in case they face it for real one Sunday. The equipment manager is thinking about how tough it's going to be to clean all those muddy jerseys.

The head coach is unique in two ways. He's the one person who sees the big picture down on the field. And he's the only one whose fate is *totally* wrapped up in winning.

If the team loses too often, the head coach will be gone.

If the team loses too often, it will fail to realize the coach's vision, no matter how many players pile up impressive stats.

With the advent of free agency and the salary cap, the National Football League fits right in with the modern business world. There is less continuity, less stability, fewer long-term guarantees than ever before. There is more turnover, more scrutiny, more emphasis on recent performance— whether in the fourth quarter or the last quarterly report. Many of your front-line people don't know if they'll stay with you next year. And the newcomers have no clue about your company's culture, about how you go about striving for success.

You can't be a team-first player until you understand what your team stands for, and that's where the leader comes in. It's my job to integrate new people into our system as quickly as I can.

As competitive pressures keep rising, the football-type organization may be eclipsed by a more efficient and flexible model. The *Wall Street Journal* compared it to a doubles tennis team. Doubles partners play certain roles—when one person serves, the other is at the net—but those roles are interchangeable. Each person must be prepared to do anything. If an opponent lobs the ball over my partner's head, I better hustle back there to return it.

If I take a me-first approach—*That's not my job*—you can bet we won't make it to Wimbledon. Doubles partners are *forced* to cooperate, all the time. As soon as they stop working together, failure is imminent.

As I look at business today, that's the kind of team we all need to build.

4.

CONFIDENCE

THE DATE: JANUARY 25, 1987.

The place: The Rose Bowl, Pasadena, California.

The game: Super Bowl XXI, Giants vs. Denver.

The scenario: We're losing by 1 point at the half. On our first series of the third quarter, it's fourth down and a yard to go on our own 39.

What do we do now? The safe and conventional play is to punt the ball, let our defense take over, and hope we get it back in decent field position. To go for the first down would be highly risky; if we failed, the Broncos would be sitting 10 yards from a shot at a field goal.

Yet something tells me this is not the time to be safe or conventional. The Giants came into Pasadena with eleven straight victories. We'd won our two previous playoff games by a combined score of 66–3; we'd been *pounding* people. But in this Super Bowl we've been strangely sluggish. In the first half Denver drove the ball for two scores, and we were hurt by some uncharacteristic penalties. We need something to wake us up. We need to *do* something.

Before the game I took aside Jeff Rutledge, our backup quarterback, and told him to be ready to use "Arapahoe." (The name stood for *A Run, A Pass, A Hit On the Enemy.*) In this special play, our team would shift from punt formation into an offensive alignment. Based on what he saw in the defense, our quarterback would then call an audible for either a run, a pass, or a quarterback sneak—our "hit on the enemy." If he didn't like what he saw, he had one more option—to take a 5-yard delay of game penalty, and *then* we'd punt.

Now, I decide, is the time. I've got a lot of confidence in Arapahoe, because we've executed it successfully four or five times that season. I also have confidence in Rutledge, a smart and heady player—and that's a good thing, since the game may hinge on what he does next. As Rutledge moves up to the line, I see him looking straight at me, as if he isn't quite sure whether to go for it. I nod my head; it looks good to me. But it's his call, his responsibility. . . .

Rutledge gains 2 yards on his quarterback sneak, and we ultimately score a touchdown on the drive. My team is revived. We've got hot dice, and we keep on rolling them. Our next touchdown is set up by a 44-yard flea-flicker, Phil Simms to Phil McConkey. The one after that is keyed by a 22-yard bootleg run by Simms. Denver can't recover; we win going away.

That game plan wasn't a departure for my teams. Four years later, in the fourth quarter of the Giants' NFC Championship game against San Francisco, linebacker Gary Reasons would take the snap on a fake punt and roll for 30 yards, setting up a crucial field goal in our eventual 2-point win. If the play fails, we lose—we give the game to them.

Last season, in our playoff game against Cleveland, with a Patriots team far less accustomed to high-pressure gambles, we used a fake punt to get a first down, leading to a field goal that tied the game at the half.

And we had plenty of other special plays prepared for that game—we just didn't get the opportunity to try them.

I've always thought that it's deadly to tighten up your game plan in the playoffs. That's the time you need to pull out all the stops. Former players of mine, long since retired, will call me up before a big one and say, "Got all your ammo ready?" They know that I'll look for an advantage anywhere I can find it—and that my team won't leave anything in the bag.

THE HIGHER THE STAKES, THE TOUGHER THE COMPETITION, THE MORE DARING YOU MUST BE TO CARRY THE DAY.

A data processing company desperately needs a new bank contract to replace a big client it has lost. It gets past the first cut; it's one of three contenders invited to present its case to the bank's vice president and his staff. Does the company play it safe with a standard, dry, by-the-numbers presentation, and hope that it squeaks by its competition? Or does it take a chance with splashy graphics and charts, and—riskier still—a live run-through, where it crunches a data set right there in the meeting?

You'd guess the odds are pretty good that if that run-through works, the contract will be theirs.

The chances my team takes are calculated—only fools gamble at random. But you can't play safe and pursue your vision; you can't shrink from risk and expect others to follow you. Too many organizations are unwilling to challenge the process, to make the big deal or develop the new product that might push them past their rivals. There are general managers in the National Football League who *never* make a controversial trade for fear of the scrutiny that would follow. They like to be regarded as "methodical." They just waddle along and hope things work out.

On the other hand, there are a like number of businesses that operate on impulse, that fail to analyze before they leap. They consider themselves "aggressive"—after all, they're *doing* something, aren't they? And they also wind up failing.

But there is a middle ground, a terrain of bold but carefully planned risk-taking. When you ask people to try something out of the ordinary, and then lead the way, it shows them that you're unafraid. And when you hand them what they perceive to be an edge on the competition, they become even more confident in your leadership. It builds a kind of mutual trust. You're trusting them to get a difficult job done; they're trusting you to do everything possible to help them succeed. The result is a stronger, more cohesive organization.

It takes time and experience to develop a positive risk-taking attitude. In my first year as head coach, I was as conservative as any of them, playing by the book. In 1984, my second year, I gained confidence as our team and coaching staff improved. By 1986 we *knew* we were good and behaved accordingly; when you've got enough talent, it gets easier to perform without a net.

Let's go back to our data processing firm. After its people hold their breath and survive that initial run-through, they'll be less fearful at their next audition. They might gain enough confidence to present even more demanding or complex presentations—which in turn will make them tougher to beat.

You can't rush this process within an organization. But strong leadership can prod it along, where weak leadership makes people risk-shy. Here are some strategies that have worked for me:

NEVER ASK PEOPLE TO DO THINGS THAT ARE BEYOND THEM. My '93 Patriots, like my '83 Giants, just weren't ready to perform at a consistently high level. My job was to keep the game close, and then we'd try to win it at the end. If I'd repeatedly asked these teams to execute plays beyond their ability, I'd have cost them the game—and hurt their confidence to take more manage-able risks in the future.

RESERVE YOUR RISK-TAKING FOR TIMES WHEN THE RISK-REWARD RATIO IS FAVORABLE. In com-ing back to win our game against Minnesota last season, we drove to a first down at their 15-yard-line in overtime. The year before, when Drew Bledsoe was a rookie, I prob-ably would have tried to run the ball a couple times, playing safe to preserve a field goal. But now my quarter-back was a little more mature, and the team had tremen-dous momentum, so I called a play-action pass and accepted the risk of an interception. We scored on that play and won the game, a confidence-booster for all concerned.

EXPLAIN WHAT YOU'RE TRYING TO ACCOMPLISH. When people understand the point of the risk, they're more likely to give their all in the effort, and less likely to second-guess afterward. Good communication expands your leadership base, as people realize that the leader's on their side, and vice versa.

PREPARE AND REHEARSE THE GAMBLE IN LOWER-PRESSURE SITUATIONS. If we hadn't tried Arapahoe during the regular season in 1986, I couldn't have had confidence that we'd pull it off in the Super Bowl. Meanwhile, my players went into that game thinking: *This crazy guy could do anything, so we better be ready to execute it.*

ACCEPT FALSE STEPS AS OPPORTUNITIES TO LEARN. It's one thing to hate failure; it's another to fear it. (Had I feared failure, I never could have taken the New England job in the first place.) When you try a play that backfires, it's always an education—either the concept was flawed, or the execution needs work, or both. If you succeed every time, you're not risking.

When taken in the right spirit, a failed risk can be a valuable lesson, even a stepping stone for the organization. In the middle of our seven-game winning streak that closed the Patriots' '94 regular season, we took on the Jets at home. Though we outplayed them throughout the first half, we led by only 10–7.

With ninety seconds to go before halftime, we get the ball back on our own 16. The prudent move would be to run the clock out, especially since we're bound to have better field position after we receive to start the second half.

But I feel exasperated. I want the score to reflect the work we've done—I'm impatient, I'm a little greedy. So I direct Bledsoe to go to our two-minute offense. On the first play he connects for a first down. On the second play he hits a short pass. On the third he forces the ball down the middle of the field, and the Jets intercept. They kick a field goal to tie it at the half.

I'm mad at Bledsoe and I'm mad at myself for my dumb decision—which makes me even madder at Bledsoe. I yell at him and he fires back; he's frustrated, too.

After we win the game, and everyone's cooled down, it's time for the lesson. I go into the locker room and tell my quarterback, "When I allow you to do something against the soundest principles of football, it's because I have confidence in your ability to get us into the scoring zone. When I do that, *you've* got to cover for *me*. You can't take the chance you took till we cross midfield. You've got to make me look good."

As soon as I said that, Drew got it. It wasn't like he'd made an idiot play anymore; he had the whole picture, and the two of us were in it together. Later in the year, when we faced a similar situation, I'd remind him, "Drew, we're trying to score here, but not at all costs." And he learned; he started calculating our risk.

When targeting errors in judgment, put them in a broader context. You'll make more headway if you explain how reckless risks damage the organization as a whole, and if you reaffirm your common purpose.

The most basic way to demonstrate confidence is by enabling people to act—by delegating authority. It starts by assembling a strong staff. In New England my offensive coordinator is Ray Perkins, who hired me back in 1981 when he was head coach of the Giants. Ray has a powerful personality; he's an outspoken, take-charge kind of guy. I never feel threatened by those qualities. I think they make our team stronger.

When you fail to give your staff meaningful tasks and input, you wind up with robots and yes-men. You stop getting quality advice and innovative ideas. Every way isn't my way. The challenge is to find the *best* way, and then collectively commit to it.

As a football coach, there's only so much you can control. You get your players ready to play and give them a design, a game plan, but it's up to them to execute it. You call a given play, but your quarterback must be free to call an audible—to change the play—at the line of scrimmage. You prepare your offensive linemen with certain blocking schemes, but you trust them to adjust and improvise against changes in the defense.

Healthy organizations constantly look to tap people into leadership positions. They don't necessarily get a title, but their contributions are well used and recognized. With the Patriots I'm very lucky to have Bruce Armstrong on my offensive line. Bruce is a Pro Bowl tackle, and he's also extremely bright in picking things up; you go over it once, and he gets it. On Sundays I breathe easier on the sideline because I know he's carrying me right into the huddle. After Drew calls the play, Bruce will throw his two cents in—"Don't be offside on this"; "Make sure you down the ball, Drew"; "Hey, we haven't got enough time to run another play."

When you head up a large or far-flung department, where you can't personally oversee everything all the time, it's essential to find and develop surrogate leaders who understand the organization's goals. These people don't have to occupy high places in the line of command. More important: the quality to influence others, regardless of the surrogate's position.

Bruce Armstrong is one of my stalwarts now, a guy I rely on, but it took a while to win his confidence. He'd seen head coaches and general managers come and go, and this was his attitude: "We've heard it all before, and nothing's ever worked." He was like a number of Patriots veterans: beaten down and cynical, almost arrogant.

When I first got to New England, you couldn't have found anyone more negative or defensive or reluctant to be taught. When my offensive line coach tried to help him correct a technique, Bruce would cut him off and explain why he'd had to solve the problem *his* way. He was usually accurate, but that wasn't the point; by acting like he knew it all, he wasn't getting the benefit of any coaching. He could understand everything you were trying to do, but he wasn't *with* you.

So Bruce was a tester, and I liked that—I enjoy the challenge of bringing a rebellious guy into the fold. And the higher the profile of the guy who's testing you, the better off you are. Because the other players see that you're not bullying around some free agent—you're fighting to lead your team, and it's out in the open.

Bruce and I needed each other. He was a building block for our program; I was his boss. But without mutual trust, I knew it was a matter of time before the relationship blew up. It happens all the time in sports. The player rebels to the point that he's no longer effective, and the coach gets rid of him, hurting the team in the process.

Then one day Bruce gave me an opening by saying, "Is there something bothering you with me?" We talked pretty hard for thirty minutes, and since then I've never had a problem with Bruce Armstrong. He's a proud man, but he didn't take offense at my criticisms. And once he responded, I could see what a huge contributor he'd be.

It also helped that we began to win some games. When you start winning, trust is easier to come by.

Whenever new management rides into Dodge, the old guard will test you. Say you work in marketing for a food manufacturer that just bought a beverage company. The toughest, brightest, most dynamic marketing guy in that beverage firm is loudly skeptical about your knowledge of their soft drinks and what makes them sell. He's stubborn, he's recalcitrant, and he doesn't back down easy.

It will do you no good to sidestep the challenge, or to slap down the ringleader as your first order of business. That will only confirm your reputation as an untrustworthy outsider—and you'll definitely aggravate the general discontent. The fact is, you *need* that ringleader. You need him to ensure a smooth transition, to help build the subsidiary's future; he could be a valued asset to the integrated corporation, and he'll pull in his colleagues behind him. It's your job to get past his doubts and convert him to your company's mission. The guy might prove to be unwinnable, and there may come a time when you'll have to part company, but you owe it to your company to give it your best shot.

In healthy organizations confidence gets infectious. When Phil Simms came to the Giants, he was a guy who played his best when he knew the organization was behind him. He needed to have his coach solid in his corner, no matter what the fans or the media might be saying that week. If Phil felt uncertain he could get tentative; he'd stop taking those positive risks.

In 1986, our first Super Bowl season, we pushed our record to 8-2 with a 17–14 win over the Eagles in Philadelphia. Simms struggled that day; several passes were dropped, and he wound up completing only six of eighteen. It didn't help that our top receivers had been hurt, on and off, the whole year. Simms had been booed at home all season. He was getting blistered by the stat-crazy press. We were winning, but we weren't winning high tech enough for people—we were winning Neanderthal.

So before our next game at Minnesota, I called Simms into my office to remind him what mattered: That we'd just beaten three tough divisional opponents in a row. That the *team* was in first place.

"Everyone's on your ass, and I don't know what you're thinking," I told him, "but I need a battlefield commander here. I need you to be the daring player you've always been. To hell with the consequences—just go out there and be daring."

With just over a minute to play in Minnesota, the Vikings led us, 20–19. The outcome might determine whether we'd hold home-field advantage through the playoffs. We were at our own 48-yard line, fourth down and 17 yards to go. The Vikings stacked their secondary with eight defensive backs. Simms dropped back, waited, got hit—and completed a 22-yard pass to Bobby Johnson. Which set up a winning field goal.

In my press conference after that game, I told the media straight out, "If any of you don't think that man can play quarterback, you're covering the wrong sport." Then Simms passed by, and I grabbed him and whispered—loud enough so that everyone could hear me—"You can play on my team anytime you want."

Sometimes it's easier to criticize than to praise. We all know that timely, constructive criticism can erase mistakes and reverse organizational decay. But it's praise that fuels a company's progress, that bolsters people's confidence and spurs them on to greater things. Winning managers *look* for opportunities to praise—for the person who stays late to finish a report, or helps seal a complicated deal, or points out a way to cut costs. The achievement doesn't have to be large or dramatic. Anything that reflects a commitment to the company is praiseworthy.

My whispered remark to Phil Simms in Minneapolis cemented our relationship. From that point on, it wasn't a question of whether we thought our team could do it—it was just a matter of how we'd go about it. And as Simms felt more secure in his role, and the team continued to win, it strengthened his confidence in the players around him, in Joe Morris and the offensive line. Our higher-risk plays no longer carried so much pressure, because there were more trusted people to carry the load.

In New York we had a number of veteran leaders, on the field and off. Harry Carson and George Martin were diplomatic and sensitive to others' feelings, but also well-respected and powerful orators. Lawrence Taylor was louder, more direct, more intimidating—but his style worked, too, because no one questioned his passion for winning. As that team developed, I learned to trust it to police itself.

Going into the '86 season, I could tell my defense wasn't primed. It just didn't have that championship edge. After we lost our first pre-season game, I'd exhausted my patience. I gave the players hell for not working hard enough. They made some minor Band-Aid adjustments, did a little better, but we still weren't ready when we opened the regular season against the Cowboys, and we lost, 31–28.

With hindsight, I realized that I should have let the team get kicked around a couple more times in pre-season before reading it the riot act. The players needed to bear the brunt of their shortcomings firsthand before they'd act to correct them.

EXPERIENCE CAN BE A BETTER TEACHER THAN ANY HARANGUE—IF YOU TRUST PEOPLE TO LEARN FROM IT.

After the Dallas game Carson and Taylor told me not to worry, that they'd straighten out the problem internally. Six days later we smothered San Diego's Air Coryell team, 20–7, and we were on our way.

There's a fine line between delegating authority and turning the asylum over to the inmates. You want to be a fair, attentive, confident leader. You want to encourage people to take initiative, put forward original ideas, take the calculated risk. But if you go too far, you can wind up *accommodating* people. You can find yourself stepping back to keep the surface appearance of unity—and to avoid confrontation with people who are staging a house rebellion.

Harry Carson was one of my very greatest players, a nine-time Pro Bowler, a proud, hardworking, stand-up guy. I consider him my friend to his day. Harry always wanted to win, and before the 1984 season he told me that he wanted to assert more leadership on the team. He even asked us to buy him a film projector, so he could learn more about the game and better guide our defense.

A few weeks later, a dispute over a contract extension led Harry to walk out of training camp. He was still under contract; he wasn't authorized to leave. I understood the situation, but that didn't mean I liked it, and I was forced to fine him.

When the press came to me, I said, "It may be about a new contract for Harry, but it's about some other things for me. Harry came to me in the off-season and talked to me about wanting to be a team leader. While he's out of camp, I hope he goes to the library and looks up the term 'leadership,' so when he comes back here he has a hell of a lot better idea of what it is than he's exhibiting now."

I knew the headlines I'd be making, but I didn't care. I needed to make a very strong point to this particular player—that if he wanted to win the team's confidence in his leadership, he had to give more than lip service.

A few days later the dispute was resolved and Harry returned to camp. And he was a tremendous leader on our team till the day he retired.

In general, we tend to delegate more authority to people who've proven they can help us succeed. Which is as it should be, provided it doesn't get out of hand. Sometimes you have to go back in and tighten the reins, just to get back to base, and that's when people resent you. They see you as a Prussian general, but you're just trying to do your job.

Like loyalty, confidence within an organization has to stretch up as well as down. There are times when leaders have to tell everyone else to get out of the way. They don't always have the luxury of explaining each step they take. Once trust is established, those occasions become fewer—and better accepted.

As Al Davis once told me, "You know, there are going to be times when you're driving this train and you're in a dark tunnel. And sitting behind you are your players and your coaches, and also the general manager and the owners of your franchise. They're sitting there watching you and they're all screaming and yelling at you, wanting to know what the hell is going on.

"And there are going to be times when you just can't turn around and explain it to 'em. You've just got to drive till you get out of the tunnel—or till you wreck the train, one way or the other."

I'd just add that the best railroad engineer in the world needs a strong fireman and a sharp brakeman, and a conductor to keep some order, or he's likely to crash every time.

No one questions the importance of confidence in determining success. It's true for armies, or football teams, or businesses warring for market share. But the roots of confidence are sometimes misconstrued. People don't get it from fancy pep talks, or psychological string-pulling, or positive-thinking handbooks. An organization's confidence level is defined, first and last, by its tangible performance.

CONFIDENCE IS ONLY BORN OF DEMONSTRATED ABILITY.

In my business, a team's collective mental state is ruled by *the psychology of results.* In other words, past outcomes dramatically affect the group's attitude going into the next game. A team teaches itself what it is on the field, in action. Sometimes this can be a resource to the leader; at other times, you're fighting your darnedest to overcome it.

To keep his team on track, a coach must take this syndrome into account *before* the fact, and frame the most positive mind-set he can for his players. (As Bear Bryant once advised me, "You better know what you're gonna tell 'em if you're winnin' at halftime, and you better know what you're gonna tell 'em if you're losin'.") Coaches can't leave their teams to decide for themselves what's going on; they have to assert their influence, prepare their players for any result.

When my good Giants squads headed into a stretch of divisional play against our main rivals, I could level with them that these games would make or break our season. With a less confident team in New England, it could be dangerous to put too many eggs into one or two contests; if we lost, my players might give up the fort.

Within the psychology of results, there are four scenarios to contend with: play well and win; play well and lose; play poorly and win; play poorly and lose.

PLAY WELL AND WIN; THE DANGER OF OVER-CONFIDENCE. No matter how great a team is, it's always vulnerable when the heads get fat. We found it toughest to prepare our powerhouse Giants clubs when a heavy underdog was next on the schedule. I'd try to avert a letdown by telling my players, "Look, if we play like we did last week, this team will not beat us. But if there's just a little drop-off, and you let this team hang around, they're going to feed off their ability to stay close, and then you'll have a dogfight on your hands."

When you get that development, and I've seen it many times, the psychology of results swings right there within the contest. The two-touchdown favorite isn't mentally prepared for the dogfight, and they usually don't cope with it too well. The underdog, meanwhile, welcomes the scrap: "Gee, we can *get* those guys." They're ready to tangle and you're just reacting. They're the same old team they were coming in, but you've dropped to their level.

I would do about anything to fight off this smug

mentality. In the 1989 pre-season things were going just a little *too* well for the Giants; my players were getting cocky, sliding into cruise control. So in our last pre-season game I devised a game plan that gave them virtually no chance to win—on purpose. It was a *rotten* game plan, so bad that they got suspicious; the reins were so tight they couldn't function.

After we lost the game to Pittsburgh, 13–10, I took full advantage of my opportunity. "We really stink," I told them. "We're bad. We don't have a chance if we play like we did tonight." It gave me a chance to wake them up.

PLAY WELL AND LOSE; THE PLIGHT OF LOST CONFIDENCE. Players can react in one of two ways to this. The first is devastation: "We played as well as we could, but we're just not good enough." The second is complacency: "We really outplayed them; we just didn't get the breaks." The truth lies somewhere in between— the team may indeed have played well enough to win, but it could also have done something more, or better, to prevail.

After the first two games of the '94 season, the Patriots led the league in scoring with 70 points. Everyone was buzzing about how we'd led Miami on the road deep into the fourth quarter, or how we'd come back from a two-touchdown deficit to draw even with Buffalo, the defending conference champion. Bledsoe had shot it out with Dan Marino and Jim Kelly, Ben Coates was catching everything in sight—the whole offense was cooking.

But our record was 0-2, because my team wasn't yet able to recognize the key moments where we had to step up and rally and turn the game in our favor.

I work in a bottom-line industry. Even so, I try to avoid being hypercritical after a loss. A disciplined coach applies the same standards to evaluate each performance, win or lose, and ignores how his team is reviewed by fans or the press. (In New England the media calls me "Punxsutawnie Bill" for the way I insulate myself from outside opinions.) I know whether I've done a good job, whether my team was well prepared; the scoreboard doesn't have to tell me that.

PLAY POORLY AND WIN; THE PITFALL OF FALSE CONFIDENCE. Sometimes the bottom line traps you. When we win a game but perform sloppily, or casually, and I see my players celebrating, I find it revolting. So I confront them with what really happened out there. Maybe we got a lucky bounce; maybe we survived a dogfight we shouldn't have had in the first place; maybe the opposition was just too inept to overcome us. I warn them that we're living on borrowed time. Sooner or later, an underachieving organization runs into someone that exploits its nonchalance.

In 1993, after losing our first four games, the Patriots went into Phoenix and outplayed them all day long. With forty seconds to go, we're ahead by 2 points. The

Cardinals have no time-outs. Our halfback, Leonard Russell, makes a great run for a first down to clinch the game —except that he jumps up and exuberantly spikes the ball, which is called a taunting penalty. Now we have to punt, and Phoenix gets three more shots to set up a winning field goal.

We hung on for the win that day, but I can't forget that we made about ten ridiculous mistakes—that we deserved to lose. There were no celebrations in our locker room that day.

PLAY POORLY AND LOSE; THE PAIN OF NO CONFIDENCE. That '93 Patriots team went on to lose its next seven games, till it stood at 1-11. I knew the team was playing at a higher level than it had the year before; eight of our losses were by a total of 26 points. But it was an uphill struggle to convince my players that we were making any progress.

I've never bought the idea that you learn much from losing. In my experience, you learn far more from winning, which also makes your players more receptive to criticism. All losing does is reinforce the things that cause you to lose, and I already know what *they* are. When you're out-prepared, outplayed, outcoached, out-motivated, out-conditioned, outsmarted—can you tell me something positive you can get out of that?

Still, a coach needs to carry the torch of hope when all seems bleak around him. After each Patriots loss I'd confront the small but deadly things we'd done to blow another close game. I wasn't letting the players slide,

wasn't giving them an inch of slack. Each week of practice was more pressure-packed than the one before. The
players could tell from my behavior that we were going
forward—that I hadn't given up on them, and I wouldn't
tolerate losing ways.

We might be out of the playoffs, but I hadn't written
off the season. We had something to prove to ourselves.

My players were practicing hard and well. "You
keep doing this," I told them, "and it's going to turn for
you." The team was starting to understand how to use
the clock, when to take time-outs. By December we were
a pretty smart group—we still had limited talent, but we
knew more about the ways to win.

And we won the last four games of the year, including an overtime finale that knocked Miami out of the
playoffs. My team had taught itself that we weren't quite
as hopeless as advertised.

We weren't out of the tunnel yet, but our upturn had
bought the coach some time. The players would ride with
me awhile longer.

5.

ACCOUNTABILITY

IN 1964 I GOT MY FIRST JOB IN FOOTBALL AS ASSISTANT COACH at Hastings College in Nebraska. Hastings was a small Division III school, with rivals like Colorado Mines and Chadron State, but I thought I was coaching in the Rose Bowl every week, believe me.

Our best player at Hastings was a rough-and-tumble, hardworking guy named Jack Giddings, who played fullback on offense and safety on defense. We were heading toward our big game of the year, with Nebraska Wesleyan, which had been killing people all season with a bootleg pass play. I took a lot of time that week drilling our defense to stop it.

The first time Nebraska Wesleyan got inside our 20-yard-line, they ran that bootleg. And scored an easy touchdown on Giddings's side of the field.

Well, I was irate. Almost out of control. I got on Giddings something terrible: "Goddamn it, I went over this with you—how could you let this happen?" I ranted on for a while, until Dean Pryor, my head coach, came up and said, "Leave the player alone."

"But, Coach, we worked on this a hundred times in practice—"

Pryor stopped me cold: "Well, you didn't work on it
enough, because he didn't get it."

That cut like a knife in the heart, but it was one of the
best lessons I've ever learned. Giddings was a conscientious
kid. He put everything he had into his preparation each week.
If he wasn't able to make that particular play, it was *my* responsibility as his coach—and here I was, berating him.

The next chance I got I went to Giddings with a different
tack: "Jack, do you understand what happened here? If it
comes up again, you be ready for it." Sure enough, Nebraska
Wesleyan tried the bootleg one more time, and we covered it
perfectly.

*ACCOUNTABILITY STARTS AT THE TOP. YOU
CAN'T BUILD AN ACCOUNTABLE ORGANIZATION
WITHOUT LEADERS WHO TAKE FULL RESPONSI-
BILITY.*

Most managers have no problem in setting up criteria to
evaluate their subordinates: productivity, efficiency, time
management, appearance, and so on down the line. But sometimes they forget that scrutiny is a two-way mirror—that people look at their leaders every day, and form their opinions
based on what they see. The subordinates have fewer, less
complex criteria. They want to know whether their managers
practice what they preach—and whether they're steering the
ship, or just drifting with the wind.

If the organization hopes to move forward, those people better see what they're looking for. If a company hopes to cultivate people who are organized, astute, fearless, and responsive, it better have some leaders who can model the way.

In my business, a team reflects its coaching staff, and in particular its head coach—his personality, his behavior, what he views as fundamental to the game. I think that coaches should be judged on three things:

1) Do the players have a design that allows them to function on game day?

2) Are they prepared to deal with contingencies that may confront them?

3) Do they behave the way the coach wants them to?

Not every team has enough talent to win the Super Bowl, but any competent coach can field a team that is strategically sound, that plays with discipline, that doesn't beat itself. If any of those components are missing, it's the coach who must be held accountable.

In the twelfth game of the '93 season, the Patriots went on the road to play a decent Pittsburgh team. We were 1-10 at the time, but we gave the Steelers all they could handle. In the final minutes of the game, trailing by 3 points, we drove 94 yards to the Pittsburgh 1-yard-line. Just as the clock ran out, our prize rookie quarterback, Drew Bledsoe, plunged toward the goal line. It looked like a touchdown—except that Bledsoe forgot to extend his arms to make sure the football penetrated the end zone. The officials ruled us 6 inches short, and we lost.

I was frustrated after that game, to say the least. I told Bledsoe, "*Anybody* has enough sense to do that." But the fact was that he hadn't had enough sense. If I'd reminded him to put the ball over the goal line, he would have done it. Bledsoe made the mistake, but I had only myself to blame.

Accountable leadership isn't some mysterious quality. It starts and ends with hard work. From training camp through the end of the season, about half the year, we put in seven days a week, and a lot of those days go twelve and fourteen hours. But it's the off-season that separates football coaches. It takes a lot of time to prepare for the draft, plan your free agent signings, and supervise off-season development programs for individual players.

Some NFL coaches aren't willing to pay that price. They use the winter and spring to refuel their engines after the fatigue of the season. They'd rather be playing golf or making speaking engagements, and so they leave personnel matters to the front office. And some keep skating along, doing the bare minimum, even when the games are being played. This kind of coach is thinking, *I'll do this as long as they let me, but pretty soon they're not going to let me anymore, and that's okay.*

We all know of companies where leadership is a license to coast, to dump work on others. And we see the inevitable results: resentment, confusion, and underachievement throughout the organization.

LEADERS HAVE TO WORK HARDER THAN THE PEOPLE THEY HOPE TO MOTIVATE.

I'm not the workaholic I once was, and I treasure my vacations. But two days after the season's over, my mind begins to churn about what we can do to put next year's team together. As I see it, my accountability doesn't end with the outcome of our games and the end product we put on the field. I'm also responsible for the formation of that product, for helping to find the players we need to fulfill our vision. Which means I don't get many days off before June.

But while hard work is essential, by itself it isn't enough. A leader's style of work is equally critical. There's a big difference between *leading* and *managing*. You can manage inventories, but you lead people. You can manage from afar, with a fax machine and a cellular phone, but you better be up close and personal when it comes to leading.

A sink-or-swim sales manager might say, "Let's just give him a territory and see what he can do." Or, "Here's the stock we're trying to sell, and here's our target price—go out and beat the drum and sell it." This kind of manager doesn't steer the new sales rep to prospective clients, or warn him about the old ones' idiosyncracies. He doesn't furnish data about the product's significant features, or recent improvements, or past trouble spots. He just turns the guy loose.

More often than not, the guy's going to sink.

In the NFL we've got head coaches marching up and down the sidelines without headsets on. They're not calling the plays—they're allowing their staff to manage various segments of the game. At a pivotal point an assistant might come up and ask for guidance. But at other times the head coach may not know whether his team's about to run or pass, blitz or cover, rush or return the punt. He operates as a cheerleader, as a traffic cop. He's abdicated responsibility.

That's the quickest way to lose, because assistant coaches

instinctively bring other agendas to the table. Offensive coordinators, for example, want to gain as many yards and score as many points as possible. Though they'd say that their goal is to win, their *real* goal is to get their unit to perform at its optimal level, and sometimes that's in conflict with sound game management.

Only the head coach sees the game through a wide-angle lens; everyone else zooms in on their pet segment.

Now, there are times when you're trying to find out whether a person can perform under pressure, and so you take a hands-off stance. But for the most part, leaders can't afford to sit up in the stands, to bivouac way behind the front lines. They have to be in the fray, right down there with their troops.

Leadership is the most visible thing there is—because if it's not visible, there is no leadership. People need to know who's driving the train. If they think that the drivers aren't qualified, that too much authority has gone to less experienced or competent managers, you're going to have a little train mutiny.

I could never be a cheerleader coach. On game day I take the trip with my players—I never feel any separation from them. For every play we put in, I've processed six other possibilities. Down and distance, fronts and formations, score, clock, matchups, time-outs, substitutions—there's a constantly shifting set of variables running around in my head. I have to stay on top of all of them. My mind races from kickoff to the final gun.

I want to be responsible for calling all our plays. I *need* to be responsible, and my players need to know that I'm in charge. On Monday I'll be telling them what they did wrong the day before. On Wednesday I'll give them our upcoming game plan. On Thursday and Friday I'll structure their practice, and on Saturday I'll set the time for the bus to the airport.

Now how can I go out there on Sunday and say, "Let's go, fellas," and sit out the big dance?

In the game, as on the practice field, my voice must be heard. And in the game it better be the loudest voice. It's an advice-seeking voice, not a dictatorial voice, but it's also the decision-making voice, the one in control.

Like most businesses of the nineties, modern football has grown complex and specialized. A head coach can't survive without high-level collaboration with his staff; no one person can see everything that happens on the field. When I'm on the sideline, my headset connects me to the coordinator whose unit is on the field (offense, defense, or special teams), as well as to our backfield coach, who serves as audio messenger to our quarterback or defensive captain. In the heat of the action, that sound track can get loud and emotional, with two or three people talking at once. At times I'm torn between making a strong leadership decision and getting that extra bit of knowledge from one of my specialists.

If you look back through history, from Lincoln to Churchill, some of the boldest, most decisive moves came about after long, hard thought. It's rarely easy to make an important decision, but effective leaders keep their doubts to themselves, concealed from their organization and the public. And once that decision is made, they throw their heart and the full weight of their office behind it.

IT'S BETTER TO DECIDE WRONGLY THAN WEAKLY; IF YOU'RE WEAK, YOU'RE LIKELY TO BE WRONG ANYWAY.

When I took the job as Giants head coach in 1983, I had to choose between Scott Brunner and Phil Simms as our starting quarterback. Neither one was established. Simms was entering his fifth year in the league, but he hadn't proven he could stay on the field; he'd lost the season before to a knee injury, half the season before that to a separated shoulder. Brunner had shown some ability in filling the gap. He was a smart guy who could read the defense and had a reasonably good arm. Neither player totally sold me in training camp, but I'd seen Brunner do more, and finally I named him the starter —even though I knew, deep down, that Simms was more my kind of guy, more fiery and aggressive.

I'm not saying that this was a bad decision, but I made it the wrong way. Lacking experience, I turned to my staff for help, but they didn't want to be a strong part of the process, either. I was fudgy and reactive; I wasn't asserting myself. I was saying, "We're going to try this, see how it goes for a while." Well, it almost went good enough to get me out of this league—especially after I wavered and replaced Brunner with Simms in our fifth game. When Simms broke his hand a few plays later, I now had one quarterback out for the year again, and a second one shaken by my loss of confidence.

We were a bad team that year—we couldn't run, block, or catch, for starters—but a stronger leader might have helped us win more than three games.

Last season, more than a decade later, I think I fell down again in the Patriots' playoff game against Cleveland. I did as much to prepare us for the post-season environment as I've done with any team, and I still don't think I did enough. I wasn't adamant and urgent enough. I just assumed my young players would muster the intensity they'd need to win, and I was wrong.

Plus I made one fatal mistake. In the week before the game, I let my staff talk me into changing a few things for Bledsoe, namely the keys he'd use to read and attack the Browns' defense. Drew wasn't practicing well, but when I went back to my assistants and questioned the changes, I allowed myself to be comforted: "Just give us another day, and we think we'll have it."

But we never really got it. Bledsoe played the same way he'd practiced. We'd failed to consider that playoff pressure—and it was Drew's first taste of it—would magnify even a small change or disruption. When you start combining new elements, it rarely works out.

It would have been easy to second-guess my staff after we lost that game, but I wouldn't do it. I knew whose fault it was; I see the same guy in the mirror each morning. When I put my stamp of approval on the change, it became my responsibility. It was a serious mistake, and I'll guard against it happening again. Next time I'll hear *my* voice out as well as all the others—and give it proper attention and respect.

COLLECT ALL THE INPUT YOU CAN BEFORE BIG DECISIONS. THEN CUT OFF THE SEMINAR AND DO WHAT YOU THINK IS RIGHT.

It takes self-confidence and will to hold yourself account-able. It takes *skill*—the right approach and technique—to get others to accept responsibility.

ACTIVE ENLISTMENT. A leader convinces people to do what ought to be done. At the outset, it's dangerous to assume that they know what that is; you've got to call their attention to the task at hand. And once they find out, they often don't want to do it, because anything worth achieving comes at a price.

It's at that point that leadership must kick into high gear. You have to draw out people's talent, feed their confidence, direct and motivate and reinforce them, and sometimes salvage those who regress. It's an uneven pro-cess, rarely smooth, full of ups and downs. The best lead-ers are the ones who stick it out through slumps and disappointments, and who hold *themselves* accountable for their people's progress.

A good teacher creates an environment which allows the student to succeed; the same applies to coaches, among other managers. I can't respect a teacher who says, "I'll expose the students to the material, but it's *their* job to learn—if they get it, they get it." As far as I'm concerned, that's not teaching. A real teacher works and works to find the best way to reach a student; the com-mitment is open-ended. If that student never gets reached, it's the teacher who feels a failure.

At the same time, I have to confess that I've yet to teach anything to a person who didn't want to start to learn. There has to be a little *self* in the motivation. A good leader hunts for the button that gets the guy to want to do it, but some guys just don't have a button.

If a person is fundamentally lazy, to borrow a catch-phrase from Little League baseball, you might as well sack up your bats and head home.

NO EXCUSES. This is the big one. Excuses and alibis are the main enemies of accountability. It's human nature to rationalize about why we're not doing well. It's also a drain on the energy and ingenuity we'll need to reverse our fortunes.

In football we have whole rotating sets of excuses: too many injuries; didn't get the draft picks we wanted; got the draft picks we wanted and they turned out lousy; didn't get our players signed on time; bad calls by the officials; a green quarterback; a tough division; and that old standby, bad weather. I could write all of them down before the season started, and pluck one out whenever it became applicable.

But it wouldn't do me any good. If you can't get the job done, the best excuses in the world won't make a difference. And if you can get it done, you won't need them in the first place.

On my team we simply don't accept excuses for failure. We have this expression: "Don't tell me about the pain; show me the baby." We don't mean any disrespect to a woman's agony in childbirth. (I have three daughters myself; I have a pretty good idea about *that* process.) It's simply a way to say that we look for the result, and that the journey it takes you to get there is not that important.

This past spring, near the beginning of the NBA playoffs, my receiver coach got a call from a friend of his: Brian Hill, the head coach of the Orlando Magic. Hill was seeking a sympathetic ear. He'd just had a big fight with his best player, Shaquille O'Neal, who'd announced to his face that Hill "choked" in big games.

"Call him back," I told my receiver coach, "and tell him that nobody cares."

That sounds harsh, but it's one of the great pieces of wisdom I received from Al Davis. Personal problems, personnel problems, injury problems, drug problems, schedule problems, front office problems—nobody cares what you're up against. The sooner you put those issues out of your mind, the sooner you can direct your focus toward the *real* issue: pushing your team toward victory.

Or as Al would put it, "Just win, baby." Just win the game.

Dennis Conner, the yacht racer, has the same slant —I think he's the greatest guy I've seen in sports in the last twenty years. He doesn't always have the fastest boat, but he never alibis: "We lost, goddamn it, or we won."

Going into the Giants' '88 opener against Washington, we were hit by a barrage of injuries. My punter, Sean Landeta, was out with a pulled groin. Lawrence Taylor was suspended for a drug infraction; Carl Banks, Leonard Marshall, Mark Bavaro, all were hurt. I had about six Pro Bowl guys missing, and everybody else was pouting around. My players were pouting. My coaches were pouting. Even the local beat writers were feeling sorry for me, for our poor, hobbled Giants going up against the defending Super Bowl champs.

That's when I got *really* worried. When a team accepts too much sympathy, it has no shot—it misplaces its mission in a swamp of self-pity.

So just before this Monday night game, I went to the team and talked about the war in Vietnam, which was ancient history to most of these players. "There was one company that lost fourteen guys the first day out," I began. "But no one was sending them home. The eighty guys left had to go back out the next day, knowing full well they might lose ten or fifteen more.

"We're not losing any lives here," I went on. "Lawrence is going to be back, Landeta's going to recover. Banks and Bavaro will be better in two weeks. Right now you're getting all this sympathy, but on Tuesday morning they'll only want to know one thing: 'Who won the game?'"

After we came back that night from a 13–0 deficit to beat the Redskins by a touchdown, I entered our dressing room to find half a dozen guys chanting, "Who won the game, Bill? Who won the game?"

CLEAR EXPECTATIONS. People can't become accountable unless they understand exactly what you want. My dad was good at this when my brother and I were growing up. He was an honest guy, an excellent motivator, and he always let us know what his expectations were. He knew that we lived to play sports, but he made it clear we wouldn't play if we didn't keep our grades up.

I never had problems in school, but I wasn't the hardest worker there, either. There were times when my father frowned at my report card and said, "My expectations for you may be higher than your own, and if they are we're going to have a little problem."

If I claimed that I was trying my best, he'd shake his head like he was stunned. "What do you *think* you're supposed to do?" he'd say. "You don't get any medals for trying."

I say the same things today to prod players to reach their potential. And we also make clear to our rookies just what it will take to make our team. From our very first meeting, I try to integrate them into our system of expectations.

First, does the player know what to do? Rookies have to earn their way into pre-season games. If a running back doesn't know his blitz pickups, and he makes a mental error that springs a linebacker loose to hit Drew Bledsoe, our season could be over right there. I'll have a team rebellion on my hands if I have a rookie in there who doesn't know what to do.

Second, is he trying to do his job the way we tell him to do it—is he coachable?

Third, how consistently does he function?

Fourth, is he in condition? If not, a lack of stamina will eventually keep him from functioning at a winning level.

Fifth, is he dependable? Does he show up on time for meetings? Can he put personal distractions aside to become a dependable worker?

And sixth, does he have the talent to succeed in the NFL?

In an ideal world, the only criterion that would shape our roster is the last one. If a player couldn't perform a task, we'd either change the task or bring in a more talented player. It would be that simple.

In the real world, I'll bet that six of my twenty-four rookies this year will fall away for lack of conditioning. And that another seven or eight will be cut for not knowing what to do. And that another handful will prove undependable. But I'll also say this—not a single one of them will leave us without knowing the reason why.

SPECIFIC RESPONSIBILITIES. George Allen, the former Rams and Redskins coach, was a great one for this. The evening before a game, he'd have ten or fifteen players stand up before the team, one at a time, to speak briefly on different points that Allen considered vital to the outcome of the game. One man might talk about the need to jam the opponent's wide receivers as they came off the line; another might address some intricacy of trap blocking against a big-time defensive end.

These speakers were taking responsibility for a specific assignment. At the same time, they were enlisting teammates to work together to get it done.

I've done similar things with my teams. In New York, George Martin was my player liaison. If any trouble was brewing, I didn't want to hear about it from some committee or group therapy session—I counted on George to give me the word.

With Reyna Thompson, our deluxe special teams player, I'd personalize the challenge. If we were playing a team with a great kickoff returner, like the Detroit Lions, I might tell him, "Thompson, you're in charge of Mel Gray this week. It's your job to negate Mel Gray—and some of you other guys better help him." There it was: public knowledge that the team would be counting on Reyna, and that they'd also have to help him succeed.

I have a young player right now named Corwin Brown. He's not the most skilled guy on the team. But he plays a key role in our punt protection, which is one of the more complex designs in pro football; you have to counter a tremendous number of defensive schemes. Brown got so good at this that at one point last year I was able to say, "Okay, Brown, you are now captain of the punt team."

This was a guy who hadn't been captain of *anything* since he'd arrived here—he was just a kid trying to survive and make the club. But now I can ask him, "Do I have to worry about the punt team this week, Corwin?"

And he'll say, "You don't have to worry about it, Coach. I'm ready—we know what to do and we'll get it done." Little dialogues like these boost the pride and confidence of an accountable player. They can also give his coach some peace of mind.

CONCRETE FOLLOW-UP. You can't make people responsible just by laying out what they need to do. You have to continually monitor and assess them, and do it as objectively as you can.

In football we have an advantage; there are no safe harbors in this game. The scoreboard gives us a summary in black and white. The game tapes expose each player to the glare of what actually happened. Even so, there's always room for excuses. People will bring in external elements if you let them: "The sun blinded me there"; "That was a wet spot on the turf."

A strong leader will preempt those alibis. I watch the tapes by myself first, early Monday morning. That afternoon I set the tone of our meeting before my team looks at them: "I've been studying this all day now, and this is what I saw—this is what I think happened." I tell them what we did well and what we need to do better, especially in places where we got away with subpar execution. Then we turn on the VCR, and we deal with reality. The players are tired, they're sore, maybe they're irritated or embarrassed, and now they have to face the music—and the music plays a lot louder on Monday than on Sunday, when an individual's performance can be obscured by the whirl of action in the game.

Through it all I struggle to be honest with myself. It's not enough for my team to have a winning record, or for the press and the fans to be happy. As I see it, I've done a good coaching job if my team has reached its potential. I hold myself accountable for nothing less.

There's a rising mentality in professional sports that says: *It's never the player's fault.* You hear it regularly from the player's agent, and sometimes from the front office. When you start hearing it from the player himself, you have to jump on it. If a player won't shoulder responsibility, he won't work on his weaknesses, which means that he won't improve. He'll be constantly on the prowl for a fall guy or a scapegoat, and his teammates will resent him.

In an accountable organization, a leader must be willing to play the lightning rod—to take one for the company. But there has to be accountability from below as well, or buck-passing becomes epidemic.

When you have an employee who's sharp and productive, but who will cover his ass at all costs, you've got a problem. This guy never says, "How do we fix it?" His chorus goes like this: "It's never my fault." It's always Jamie in production who didn't get him the estimates in time, or Steve in shipping who sat on the order. Even if he's right, he's not helping the organization—and he's clearly not helping Jamie or Steve do their jobs better. (Habitual buck-passers, in fact, have a vested interest in the *failure* of others; if everyone else is doing a good job, they'll have no one to blame.)

In football there are times when it's the coach's fault, and times when it's the player's fault. A real team will recognize both of those times; real *guys*, who are real in pursuit of what they're chasing, will stand up and take what's coming, good or bad.

My better Giants teams were accountable from top to bottom, but a few people stood out. Maurice Carthon, our unsung blocking back, was off the charts. Maurice never missed a practice, never missed a game—he was always there for you. He was our sergeant at arms, a bottom-line guy who's brought the same spirit to my coaching staff in New England.

You can't win in the NFL without an out-front quarterback, someone who can handle the burden and the blame. He's got to accept responsibility for the entire offense, even in circumstances beyond his control. And he has to model the way on the field; if your quarterback isn't a fighter, if he doesn't show strong resolve, if he isn't mentally tough, your team will fold every time.

We were lucky to have Phil Simms. He wasn't a prima donna. He was a quarterback with a lineman's personality, a hard worker who'd be the last one out of the weight room. Most important, he never made excuses for failure—*never* made excuses. He stood up and took his hits, on the field and off.

But early in Phil's career there were a few times when the responsibility was too much for him. In 1984 we played Kansas City in a must game to nab a wild card into the playoffs. And we can't get Phil to do what we need to do. He's with the game plan, but he won't pull the trigger on our downfield passing plays—he's dumping the ball off or throwing it away. From the sideline his receivers look open. From up in the booth my offensive coordinator, Ron Erhardt, is telling me: "Bill, it's there—Phil's not watching the same game we're watching." But Phil is saying, "I didn't like it; I didn't see it. It wasn't there." He's not a dishonest kid. He's telling me that he's risking an interception if he goes through with the play.

This goes on into the fourth quarter, and by then we're losing 27–14. People are leaving for home; the stands are half-empty. Remember, we haven't won anything yet, and this team has made the playoffs just once in twenty years. The fans are giving up out of habit.

With eight minutes left I bring my quarterback over and I

say, "Philip"—I'm serious, now—"Philip, I'm going to take all the responsibility from you, but I want you to do *exactly* what I'm going to tell you to do. And if it doesn't work and you throw an interception, don't worry about it. I'll take all the blame." Then I tell him, "We're going to get a slot-out, and I want you to throw it to Zeke."

This is as elementary as you can make it. As coaching strategies go, it doesn't seem very bright; the Chiefs could put three guys on Zeke Mowatt, and then we'd be finished. But I'm thinking this is one time I have to number the dots for Phil, or he won't be able to connect them.

We get the ball on our 20, and we score in five plays— four of them passes to Mowatt. With two and a half minutes left, we get the ball back, and it's bang, bang, bang—Phil does it again. We win the game, 28–27, and at the end the air is filled with a jubilant honking of horns. It's the fans who'd left early, now stuck in a traffic jam, cheering the rally they've heard on their radios.

By taking the burden off Phil, I enabled him to see what the rest of us were seeing. Once he saw it, he exploited it to the max—the light went on and he had it. The curtain went up. The block disappeared. That comeback gave all of us tremendous impetus to go forward; it was a turning point for that team.

ACCOUNTABLE ORGANIZATIONS GIVE PEOPLE ROOM TO OPERATE. BUT WHEN PEOPLE FLOUNDER, THE ACCOUNTABLE LEADER DOESN'T SIT BACK AND WATCH THEM FAIL. HE STEPS IN AND

ASSUMES RESPONSIBILITY, AND STRENGTHENS THEM FOR THE NEXT TIME.

True leaders stand up to be counted in crunch time. Rather than run from the heat of a demanding job or tough judgment, they welcome it; they understand that it comes with the territory. Say you're running a software development outfit that has been built around a successful spreadsheet program. The grapevine reports that a competitor will be coming out with a more advanced product in six months. If your company doesn't counter, and fast, you'll be taking a direct hit on your market share.

Do you set up a task force to analyze the situation and return with a polished set of recommendations? Do you dump the crisis on your top technical people and tell them to work round the clock till they come up with the next generation of your spreadsheet software? Or do you turn the entire business upside down, from research to sales, to fend off the challenge —with you at the center, guiding every phase of your company's response?

In the life cycle of any business, there are a few critical moments that a leader must face, a few mammoth undertakings that only the person in charge can pull off. Those are the times that you must dive in and *do* it; the only failure lies in not taking the plunge.

6.

CANDOR

WHEN PEOPLE DON'T KNOW WHAT THEIR BOSS IS THINKING, THEY assume the worst. *My promotion is dead, our proposal was deep-sixed, the pink slip is coming*—when communication is weak, an organization's morale is bound to suffer.

It's the same on a football team. When players don't know what the coach is thinking, paranoia sets in. I've always found it best to talk straight out to them. I never lie to my players, never skirt the issue, never sell them a line or pay them false compliments. I just tell them the truth as I see it. They may get sick of my needling or pressure. They may think I'm unfair or plain wrong. But they don't tune me out; they appreciate that they're getting an honest opinion.

Leaders are watched every minute by the people around them. In my business I have eleven assistant coaches, three trainers, two equipment men, two video guys, a couple field managers, the public relations director and a few front-office types, plus fifty-six players—that's eighty people whose eyes are on me every day I walk in here. Every one of them is checking me out, because they're all going to interact with me that day in one form or another.

And it's not just what I say that they interpret; it's my attitude, my tone of voice, my body language. I may *choose* to look angry or distraught, but it has to be calculated, and it has to be an honest feeling at the same time. You can't create a charade out there.

Candor is also the rule when middle managers deal with higher-ups. (NFL coaches, take my word for it, are the ultimate middle managers.) These executives are *looking* for direction from people at the front line. My owner wants a strong leader; my general manager needs me to be explicit about the personnel I want for our team, so that he can try to get them. Sugarcoating an issue won't help. They need the straight dope —and I do my best to give it to them.

When you're evaluating people's performance, timing is everything. Every game presents issues to be resolved, weaknesses to be shored up, mistakes to be corrected. These are all essential tasks for the coaching staff, but by and large they can wait till Monday.

The worst thing you can do to a player immediately after a game is to call attention to the errors he just made. If the team won, you're spoiling a celebration, a needed release from the tension of the week. If the team lost, you're pouring gasoline on a fire—because that's when the players are most sensitive, the coaches are most emotional, and the media is most ferocious. In the aftermath of a loss, critiques can easily degenerate into finger-pointing sessions, into the assignment of blame.

WHEN SENDING A MESSAGE, IT'S NOT ENOUGH TO BE HONEST AND ACCURATE. THE IMPACT OF THE MESSAGE WILL HINGE ON WHO'S RECEIVING IT—AND WHAT THEY'RE WILLING TO TAKE IN AT THAT TIME.

When a construction firm loses out on its bid for a contract, postmortems can be instructive. Maybe a materials guy didn't check out enough places to find the highest-grade ore at the lowest cost. Maybe the engineer got too immersed in his own work, got lost in expensive perfectionism. Or maybe it was a little of both. While the head of the firm must examine these possibilities, he won't accomplish much by bawling out his employees in front of their peers an hour after receiving the bad news. They're already feeling bad about it—it's *their* work that was rejected, after all. The boss will make more headway in correcting the problems in private, after everyone's had a chance to cool off.

When our football team shuts the locker room for five minutes after the game, we circle the wagons. I'm not harping on anything that just happened on the field; I'm warning my team what the reporters will be asking them. And if one player had a really bad day, I'll point right at him and add, "They're coming after you, so be careful what you say. And you other guys better shield him."

In my own dealings with the media, I try to be honest,

and to answer every fair question; I like a lot of these guys, especially the sharp ones, and enjoy the jousting that comes with my job. On the other hand, I feel no obligation to tell them everything I know.

The media today *lives* to cast blame, and that's where I'm most guarded. Now, if a player fumbled four times and your opponent recovered three of them, you can't deny that those fumbles affected the outcome. So you've got to tell the reporters, "There's a couple plays old Joe would like to have back," or, "There's some carelessness coming out of our end zone." But you never say, "Old Joe blew the game today." You can tell the truth without driving a stake into a player's heart.

And I'm very reluctant to discuss injuries. Once you get into that area, the media forms its own opinion on a player's ability to function; it creates an excuse for that individual. There's a widely held assumption that if players can't perform at 100 percent, they shouldn't be asked to perform at all. I can tell you that in the National Football League there are very few people at 100 percent three weeks into the season—and that the teams that overcome their collective bruises and sprains are the ones that win.

After all, we don't impose that 100 percent standard on members of the media. If we did, the press box would be a lonely place on game day, especially if we barred writers for hangovers.

The media isn't an issue for most businesses, but external scrutiny can rear its ugly head anywhere. A toy company is hit by a safety recall of its top-selling tricycle, and suddenly everyone's an expert about everyone else's job. Design people are screaming about lax supervision at the manufacturing plant. The procurement guys find five major flaws in the tricycle's design. If the managers at the company want to hang on to their good performers, they'd better shield them from outside criticism—even as they conduct their own internal assessment of what went wrong.

As his career progressed, Phil Simms became very adept at handling reporters. In 1990 the Giants had won our first seven in a row before we traveled to Indianapolis for a Monday night game. The Colts weren't very good that year, but it was a perfect setup for us to get beat: national television, a noisy stadium on the road, an underdog with nothing to lose. I'm concerned we'll come in dull, so I'm on my team unmercifully all week in practice.

We come out ready to go. By the second quarter we're up 17–0, but I want one more score before halftime; with our defense, a 24–0 lead is all she wrote. We vary our attack by putting David Meggett in the game alongside Rodney Hampton—and then Phil throws the ball to the wrong place, and our drive stalls.

When he comes back to the bench, I'm irate. Phil knows he's made a mistake as well as anyone, but instead of buttoning my lip, I go after him: "What the hell are you doing?"

It's unusual for me to challenge Phil right in front of the team, and he doesn't like it, not when we've got a good lead and he's played a solid half. So he fires back: "*You* go out there and throw it!"

I'm getting madder, and I yell at him, "If you just would do what the hell you're supposed to do—*you* play quarterback, and let *me* coach the team." At this point Phil walks past me; he wants out of this fight. But I have to get in the last word: "You go sit your ass over on the bench!"

Now I've got my other players concerned, with Ottis Anderson and Maurice Carthon throwing my own words back at me: "Bill, Bill—you tell us we got to be a *team.*"

"We're going to be a team," I reply, "as soon as I finish yelling at this SOB."

TRUE CANDOR IS THE MEASURED TELLING OF THE TRUTH, NOT THE OPEN VENTING OF RAGE.

Of course, our charming byplay is picked up by the TV cameras, and I know it's going to be topic number one for the press. As we walk off the field—we win comfortably, 24–7—I catch up to Phil and give him a little pat and say, "You better be ready as soon as you walk in there about this little dispute we had."

"I'm ready," he says. "I'm going to say that I said it was less filling, and you said it tastes great." And that's what he tells the press, and it defuses the whole issue.

The next day I meet Phil in the locker room; it's time for some damage control. I tell him, "I shouldn't have said what I said to you, but you should have thrown the ball where you're supposed to."

"Aw, I know it," he says, sounding sheepish, and that was the end of it. I wasn't proud of my behavior, but Phil and I could slough off a few minutes of friction without any damage. That's what fans misunderstand—they see the ten-second camera flash, but they don't see the day-to-day partnership, the trust built over weeks and seasons, between coach and quarterback. Phil knew I'd always been straight with him, even when I went over the top.

In high-pressure environments, lost tempers are commonplace. At the commodities exchange, for example, it's no high crime for a manager to scream at one of his traders in the heat of the moment. What matters is what happens next; as the marriage counselors will tell you, you never want your partner to go to bed mad. Once that screaming manager regains control, he needs to settle the dispute quickly, to issue a calm apology and join in a rational review of events.

When we play on Sunday, Monday afternoon is the time for postmortems—for my state of the union, followed by a detailed videotape review of the game. By this time the players have heard lots of loose voices weigh in on their performance, from their agents to the beat writers and columnists and TV smile guys. Now they need to hear *the* voice—my voice, representing a unified coaching staff. And that voice better tell them the truth, the stone-cold facts, or it won't hold the team together.

This is especially important when a team is going badly. When you're losing in the NFL, this game is pure misery for everyone involved. Discussions turn adversarial. It's human nature to stick up for yourself or your group—to protect your own and get caught up in the assignment of blame. Who caused you to lose? A struggling team never lacks for targets.

"What was that defensive coordinator doing, blitzing in that situation?"

"We've got to throw the ball more on first down, everybody knows that."

"I could run back here if those guys up front would block a little bit."

"I was wide open on that pattern but Drew just didn't get me the ball."

While every Monday is different, I try to follow these guidelines:

KEEP YOUR SPEECHES SHORT. Some leaders use their meetings as a bully pulpit, but I think they bump into diminishing returns. My job is to pinpoint what we did well and what we need to work on, and I usually speak for ten or fifteen minutes. If the news is really bad, and I need to snap my team out of it, I might stand up there for half an hour, but that's the exception.

AIR OUT YOUR PROBLEMS BEFORE THEY FESTER. It does no one any good to have me stalking the practice field all week with *that look*, when we haven't dealt with whatever's bothering me. Sometimes I'll let an issue ride for a while in the hope that a player will take care of it, or the circumstances will change. But you can't let it go on forever.

DON'T TRY TO TELL THEM EVERYTHING YOU KNOW. If you bombard people with information, you'll soon put them on overload, and they won't absorb any of it. I try to pick out three or four points that are most relevant to the game tapes, and concentrate on them. One week it might be the 80 yards we lost on penalties; the next time it could be our six turnovers—or six sacks by our defensive line.

NOT EVERY EMPLOYEE NEEDS TO HAVE THE COMPANY'S BIG PICTURE IN TOTAL FOCUS. BUT THEY DO HAVE TO UNDERSTAND THEIR ROLE IN HELPING TO REACH THE LEADER'S VISION, AND TO BE CONVINCED TO WORK IN THE RIGHT DIRECTION.

NO SECRETS. There are no taboos when we talk about our team; we hold nothing back, and we use the tapes for objective corroboration. With everything exposed, there are no doubts as to why we are where we are, no question as to who deserves credit or blame. So when a player runs into some contrary opinion on the outside, he can shrug it off—just as I'd shrug off a suggestion by my barber that we need to put in a statue-of-liberty play.

KEEP IT INSIDE THE FAMILY. The only honest meetings are private meetings, and our Monday get-togethers are exclusive. Only players and coaches are invited, and our privacy is sacred; even our owner is barred. Secretaries, trainers, equipment men, the p.r. director—none of them sets foot in that room, though not for lack of trying. I know how gossip turns into rumors, and rumors into controversies, and we've already got enough of those.

What's more, we all understand that what's said in that room *stays* in that room. We don't have backbiters on my team, and that includes the head coach. If I say one thing to a player's face and another to the front office, I have a serious credibility problem.

WASHING DIRTY LAUNDRY IN PUBLIC IS PROBABLY THE QUICKEST WAY TO DIVIDE YOUR TEAM FROM WITHIN.

NO IMMUNITY FOR THE RICH AND FAMOUS. When something's going wrong, it's usually a team-wide or unit-wide problem, and we address it as such. But sometimes an individual is letting the others down, and everyone needs to hear it said: "We've got to hit harder than that, son"; "I know you're a better player than you're showing us here." And when one man's glaring mistake did indeed cost us the game, I acknowledge as much. But I also put it in perspective: "Look, old Joe had a little tough luck with this one, and it won't happen again—but think back about what this guy's done for the team, and all the plays he's made."

On a given Monday my target might be Drew Bledsoe or Ben Coates. The only ones who get any benefit of the doubt are veterans who've put in years of conscientious performance. I might take these guys aside for a few words of encouragement, or simply remind them in the meeting: "Make sure you pay attention on this; you got beat on it last week."

BE HARD ON YOURSELF. If I believe I cost my team an opportunity, if I called a play out of impatience or recklessness, I apologize. "Don't let me do this again," I'll tell them.

Confident leaders freely admit their own mistakes. And by doing it publicly, they set an example for others to take responsibility.

Candor can be positive as well as negative, a point that can get lost within troubled organizations. Once again, it's always healthy to praise a deserving unit or individual, as both reward and reinforcement.

In football this can happen naturally after a win. When the Giants drove toward a championship in 1990, Jumbo Elliott was an up-and-coming offensive tackle. In our first play-off game, against Chicago, Elliott had to block Richard Dent, a high-profile player who'd been a thorn in our side for years. Though past his prime, Dent was still very capable, but Elliott overpowered him that day. You could see it from the sideline —there were holes you could drive a bus through. We clobbered the Bears, 31–3. As usual, I had little to say in the locker room: "Nice going, we got San Francisco next week, let's get ready to go for those guys."

And then I just blurted out, "Jumbo, you are an *ass-kicker.*" That was my compliment, my whole speech. And Elliott got piled on by his teammates like the hero he was. Offensive linemen can get ignored by the fans and media, but they're highly valued by their coaches. I suspect Jumbo has never forgotten that moment.

PRAISE CAN BE MOST VALUABLE WHEN IT'S MERITED BY SOMEONE WHOSE SUPPORTING ROLE IS OFTEN OVERLOOKED.

After a law firm wins a big case, the partners who argued it in court never lack for credit. But a wise managing partner will share the champagne with the firm's associates and paralegals—the people who burned the midnight oil to dig out case law and give the partners' arguments a sound foundation.

There are times when my praise is highly calculated. After Ben Coates caught eight passes in a game last season, I addressed him at our Monday meeting: "You were great yesterday, son. They're not going to let you go free like that again. You better be prepared for some change in the defense —'cause if I'm coaching against you, you're not catching *any* passes next Sunday." Here was praise linked to a challenge, and to a piece of information the player needed to keep doing his job.

Phil Simms always said I stinted on praise. I'd tell him he did a pretty good job, then call his attention to four things I didn't like. It wasn't that I was trying to humble Phil. But starting pro quarterbacks are thrust into a fantasy world; the recognition is far too lavish, the attacks mean-spirited and unfair. While Phil managed to keep an even keel, the scrutiny he received—at both ends of the spectrum—was unreal. But what he got from me was *real*. We both knew that we both *knew*, that we understood what was true in our game. It was my job to keep him connected to that.

Drew Bledsoe probably feels the same way today, that my

compliments are few and far between. In fact, I've looked for opportunities to praise him from the start—both to keep up his own morale, and to bolster the confidence of his teammates behind him. Toward the end of Drew's rookie season in '93, after the debacle in Pittsburgh where he threw for five interceptions, I thought he raised his level of concentration and preparation. He started helping us win some games, and I was eager to point that out.

But I also give Drew the criticism that I think he needs. We've had to force-feed the kid, under pressing circumstances; my delivery can be so abrupt that it has to hurt Drew's retention. But there are times in this game when you can't worry about people's feelings, when you just have to *do* something to wake them up and restore their attention to the task at hand. And sometimes it takes a cherry bomb.

On the Friday of the last week of that '93 season, we were drilling our two-minute offense, and it wasn't going very well. Friday is a bad day for problems, because you've got no time left to fix them before the game. My patience was short, and I snapped at Drew, "You're supposed to be a pro quarterback, and you're acting like a damn high school quarterback!"

Two days later Drew threw for more than 300 yards against Miami. Toward the end of regulation he ran our two-minute offense like Roger Staubach, and connected on his third touchdown pass to send us into overtime. Then he hit his fourth touchdown to win the game. He threw just one interception all day.

When I got into the dressing room I turned to my quarterback and said, "Hey, Bledsoe, you acted like a pro quarterback today." After I added a few words to my team, Bruce Armstrong walked by me and said, "Well, Bill, I guess he skipped college, huh?"

I couldn't argue the point; the man had spoken the truth.

Our team meetings aren't free-for-alls, but they are open forums. It's not just me and my coordinators talking. As long as they stick to our agenda, anyone with something useful is welcome to jump right in. Some players are especially sharp in bringing information from the field to the meeting room or the sideline. If they tell you why a play is breaking down, or where an opponent is vulnerable to attack, you can take it to the bank. Maurice Carthon and Zeke Mowatt were like that in New York; Bruce Armstrong is the same way in New England.

But people will volunteer this help only if you've created a good rapport, an easy flow—even if it's a hot-tempered flow at times. If they get shot down for making suggestions, if the manager sits up there like a French king, the employees will clam up and do it all by the numbers. If you say, "We're going to do this job, A-B-C-D," they'll do it just that way, because their job is to please you. They'll stick to A-B-C-D even though they harbor a terrible suspicion that it should be going A-D-C-B. Even as they watch their organization go under.

TO GET HONEST INPUT, REWARD IT WITH CONSISTENT ATTENTION—AND AN OPEN MIND.

As your company's chief financial officer, you're chairing a planning meeting for the next fiscal year. Halfway in you notice that a middle manager from accounting has quietly floated some smart ideas about restructuring the budget. The restructuring would contradict the way things have been done for years, and add some short-term work to the process. You have the power to override the middle manager, to crush his brainstorm with the power of your office and company tradition. But you give his proposals an open airing instead; without new ideas, you know that the organization will stagnate.

Coaching is an act of communication—of explaining what you want of people in a way that allows them to do it, assuming they have the ability. I've lasted as long as I have in this business because I'm able to reach my players, to hear and be heard.

When I was younger, I turned every discussion into a contest—with my staff, my team, my wife. This makes life exciting, but it leads to problems. If one side always wins—whether from superior logic, or a louder voice, or simple authority—the other side goes into a shell. The communication deteriorates.

I've grown less combative in my middle age, and less impulsive. A young coach takes on five crises a day; an experienced coach pinpoints the one that will most affect his team. I won't pick a fight these days unless I'm sure of the outcome ahead of time.

I've also learned that the less you say in haste, the less you have to take back. Instead of lashing out, I try to quiet down instead. I withdraw. That can be hard on my players, too, because now they're in the dark. It's a fine line; I have to let them know where I stand, yet I have to be careful.

I'm not saying that leaders should avoid all displays of

anger. I am saying that they need to consider the consequences in advance, and have some sound intent behind them, even if the display itself seems spontaneous. In 1986 the Giants closed out their regular season at home against Green Bay. We were 13-2, and had clinched home-field advantage through the playoffs. Green Bay was 4-11. It's a meaningless game. But I don't want my team to let down going into the playoffs, and I tell them, "Listen, let's not give these guys a chance to beat us today. Let's put the pressure on 'em and get this thing over with fast."

My team responds. By the second quarter we're up 24–0. But it's too easy; we stop playing. Green Bay passes for one touchdown, returns an interception for another, kicks a field goal. Suddenly it's 24–17. The momentum has turned. The Packers are breathing fire, and we cannot stop them. If there's no halftime break, they're going to beat us 38–24.

Worst of all, my team isn't even behaving like it feels threatened. They're starting to get frustrated, but they're still ahead. They figure they can turn the switch on whenever they need to.

I'm disgusted—the whole display is making me sick. I'm *enraged* with my defense. This is a very good unit, my pride and joy, and we're getting our asses kicked.

The first thing I do at halftime is to tell my staff to stay away from the team—to make their adjustments in their head, and get out of the locker room. I'm not sure what I'm going to do, but I'm determined to snap these guys out of it. So I burst into the defensive meeting room, and I see this 55-gallon plastic barrel. It's full of paper, Coke cans, snuff, dip cups, tape—all the garbage of the week.

I start in by letting my players know what I didn't like out there, which was just about everything. I'm barking at them, really going at it. "That was the worst display of football I've ever seen," I tell them . . . and then I pick up the barrel and hurl all this stuff over the first two rows. I get about eight players. I shout at them, "You guys belong in here with the rest of the garbage!" Then I bang the barrel off a wall and storm out of the room to let them stew.

I imagine that some of those players were thinking, *The coach really lost it.* And they'd have been right, because I hadn't planned what I'd done. But—and this is critical—I had some logic behind me. I knew my players could try harder; I was appealing to their inner pride. Plus I had a confident, emotional team, with some very volatile characters, and I was one of them. They weren't easily cowed, but I woke 'em up that afternoon. The yelling was nothing special, but the garbage can was something extra—it was effective *because* it was out of character. They'd never seen me act that way before.

We outscored Green Bay 31–7 in the second half, and won going away. As I recall, we played some pretty fair defense.

You have to be judicious with scorched-earth verbal assaults. They work best when the collective confidence level is high, but *before* complacency has eroded too far—as in the pharmaceutical company that still boasts the top-selling antacid, but whose market share has slipped two quarters in a row.

My tirades are reserved for special cases, and special people. You have to know who can take it. There are times when a leader needs to be quiet and reassuring, or deliberate and explicit. There are times when you need to challenge people without bashing them over the head.

Nine games into the 1994 season, my second with New England, our record stood at 3-6. We'd dropped four games in a row; if we lost one more, the Patriots would likely fall short of the playoffs for the eighth straight year. To make it tougher, our next game was against Minnesota. The Vikings were 7-2, and they had the most prolific pass rush in the league; they'd already knocked about five quarterbacks out of action.

After the first half we were getting killed, 20–3. Our whole season was going down the tubes. I'm not feeling mad or belligerent, but I'm deeply disappointed, because we're not acting like we care about winning. It seemed like we'd given up; I couldn't see one guy who's really fighting. I was watching these players file into the locker room, in shell shock, their eyes glazed over. I could tell what they were thinking: *Here we go again* . . . And I was saying to myself, "Did I miscalculate? Have I slipped that much in judging talent? How many of these guys shouldn't even be here? Where is this team going?"

I was having one serious crisis of confidence, right there.

But leaders don't have the luxury of surrender. I had to do something, though I doubted I could make a difference that day. It wouldn't have helped to scream at these players, even if I'd been in the mood. This was a fragile bunch, with no foundation of achievement to prop it up. If I'd berated them as gutless quitters, they might have believed it; I might have crushed them.

Instead, I slowly looked around the room. I stared

straight into the eyes of my strongest veterans, guys like Vincent Brown and Bruce Armstrong, and I said very quietly, very low-key, "How long are you going to take this around here? You been here for seven years, Brown, how long you going to take it? You been here for eight years, Armstrong—you going to take it for ten?

" 'Cause if you want to take it for the rest of the season, just let me know, and that's fine with me. But don't call yourself professional football players. If you're willing to take this stuff, this isn't a team and this isn't professional football. It's just some guys out there passing the time of day and getting paid."

As I left the dressing room, I reminded them that we'd receive the ball to start the second half. I said we'd go to our two-minute offense, which I'd never, *ever* done that early in a contest. And the last thing I said was one of my standards: "We still have time to win this game."

We stuck with that two-minute, no-huddle, all-passing offense throughout the second half. It might have backfired. The Vikings could have intercepted us off the bat, pushed their lead to 27–3, and effectively ended the game—and our season. But I didn't think we had much to lose. There was no way we'd have won with our conventional offense, not with our players resigned to defeat. The two-minute drill forced the team to be aggressive, to damn the torpedoes, to push ahead whether or not they believed they had a chance.

I'd also noticed that Minnesota hadn't responded too well when we'd run the same offense at the end of their first half. Their vaunted pass rush looked a little tired. So I decided to play my hunch.

We came back from the dead to win that game in over-time. Bledsoe threw seventy passes, fifty-three of them after halftime. By the end of the game, the Viking defenders were so exhausted that they collapsed in the middle of the field—they couldn't make it to their locker room.

And our offensive line hadn't allowed one sack, or in-curred a single holding penalty, all day.

That game was a big flip for us, the springboard to a seven-game winning streak that pushed us into the playoffs. I don't know that my halftime presence turned the tide, but it did get people's attention. It worked for the same reason my tirade worked in New York: My players knew that we were on the same side. They'd learned to *listen*, because they knew I'd never lie to them. They knew that the truth would help us win, even if it hurt.

7.

PREPAREDNESS

THE OTHER DAY, AT A GOLF TOURNAMENT FUND-RAISER, I WAS paired with a young, cherubic-looking guy named Jeff Vinik. As we roll up to the second hole he tells me that he manages "some funds for a company."

By the fourth hole I find out that this guy is the Michael Jordan of mutual funds. He oversees $44 billion for Fidelity Magellan.

If Jeff Vinik ever wants to try a second career, he'd be a natural for coaching. He understands pressure; he's got to perform every single day. Most of all, Jeff knows the value of preparation. He gets to his office two hours early every morning to read, study, and analyze, before hitting the floor to make his trades. His workday ends six hours later, when the market closes, and Jeff goes home to his family. He plays with his kids until 8 P.M., and then he reads and studies for *another* three hours.

That's five hours of preparation for every six hours of

work—and that doesn't include the mound of material that Jeff takes home each weekend.

You can't be a top performer unless you're ready for the demands of your job. On a football team, preparation instills the qualities that permit a team to win. It reminds players about critical factors in executing a particular play. And it enables the coaching staff to identify trouble spots in time to correct them.

When I played quarterback in high school, my coach, a bluff Irishman named Tom Cahill, allowed me to call my own plays. That privilege came with a price, however. Every Sunday at one o'clock I'd meet with the coach at his home to discuss the game we'd just played and the plan for the next one. I'd report what I'd seen on the field, and Cahill (who later hired me to assist him when he moved on to coach at West Point) would say what he thought the team was doing well and what we needed to do differently.

I always looked forward to those sessions. It was a way to deepen my understanding of what my coach wanted to do. I was eager to please him—we both wanted to win, after all— and it was important for me to know what he thought.

To this day, I consider preparation the most enjoyable part of my work, and the most challenging. To the extent my teams have succeeded, I'd say that solid preparation—not talent or strategy—was the primary factor.

I think the same holds true in any field. If you're trying to sell big-screen televisions, you better be able to anticipate a customer's questions. It's not enough to know the obvious: size, cost, payment terms. You need to be able to talk about delivery and service, rear projection versus front projection, why one brand is better than others, what special features are on the remote control. And you need to do it without fumbling, or running every minute to the manual or your supervisor.

We don't want our football players to think during a game, because thinking takes too long. We want them to *react* —to have the correct moves so ingrained in practice that instinct guides them to the right place at the right time. It's like giving a speech; it's the drudge work and research you put into it beforehand that lets you make your points with freewheeling assurance.

THE MORE YOU PREPARE BEFOREHAND, THE MORE RELAXED AND CREATIVE AND EFFECTIVE YOU'LL BE WHEN IT COUNTS.

In the NFL we begin formal preparations in July, at training camp. It's then that our team gets ready for the grueling season to come—not just by learning the play book, but by making an *investment*, by setting its stake in the ground. In football that's mostly a physical investment. It's practice on hot days when everybody else is on vacation. It's hard and tedious work, with bruises and blisters and aching hands.

There's no substitute for that ordeal. If you just go through the motions, if your team isn't in real good condition, if your preparation is haphazard, then you haven't paid the price. Most players will take the easy road if you let them. By the time they find out it leads nowhere, it's too late.

But if everyone follows through and makes the investment in camp, a bond forms among players and coaches. It pulls people together, and it makes them stubborn. Two or four or six months later, when they're in a touch scuffle and the score is against them, they'll be thinking: *We've sacrificed to be good, and damn it, we're not giving in.*

A team's practices will predict its performance just about every time. And of all the coaches I've gone up against, the one who did the most to prepare his team was Joe Gibbs. Our Giants teams were fortunate against Gibbs's Redskins, going 11–6, but Washington was never easy to beat. They weren't going to hand you the game, and you had to finish it out. If there were forty-five seconds left in the fourth quarter, you still had to worry that something might happen. A Joe Gibbs team would *always* be ready to strike if given the opportunity.

I like to think that our team functioned the same way. In 1986, in the days leading to our first Super Bowl, we were almost getting paranoid about things going so well in practice. I was starting to say, "God*damn*, let's not leave it here on the practice field." As it turned out, I had nothing to worry about.

Unfortunately, the same syndrome works in reverse. Whenever I send my team into a game with some new wrinkle or adjustment they aren't fully prepared for, it blows up in my face more often than not. The odds are worst when the team is inexperienced, and I'm depending on "groove" players who need a well-worn track during the maelstrom of a game. In my first year with the Patriots, in a game against Buffalo, we'd been running a little toss play to the weak side. Then one of the players involved talked us into altering the way we blocked for it; he thought the change would help him take out his man. My veteran Giants players could have made that adjustment midstream. My younger Patriots players were in over their depth. The next time we ran our sweep, all *three* of our guys missed their blocks, and we got thrown for a 5-yard loss.

The repercussions were more serious in the Giants' 1989 playoff game against the Rams. After dominating the first two quarters, we were ahead by only 6–0 with less than two minutes to go in the half. They punted us back to our 15-yard-line, and we were going against the wind. My gut feeling was to run out the clock. But after two draw plays gained about 20 yards, my frustration got the better of me; I decided to take a chance and throw the ball with just twenty-five seconds left. Simms's pass was tipped by a defender and intercepted, which set up a Los Angeles touchdown and gave them a 7–6 lead at the half.

We ultimately lost that game in overtime, 19–13, and my impatience was part of the reason why. It was also the only time in my career where a bad call (a pass interference that set up the Rams' winning touchdown) clearly affected the outcome of a big game.

But none of that would have mattered if my team had truly been prepared that day. I didn't kick myself so much for calling the fatal pass play; sometimes you take a chance and it doesn't work out. But I felt guilty that my team wasn't able to execute the play with the care and discipline and judgment we needed in a high-pressure game. I thought I'd let my players down. Ever since then, I've tried to *over*-prepare my team in similar situations.

And then, in the Patriots' playoff game just last New Year's Day against Cleveland, I allowed Drew Bledsoe to come in unprepared with that new set of reads that he hadn't mastered in practice.

When people talk about not making the same mistake twice, I've got to laugh. If I never made the same mistake twice, I'd be the most successful coach in the history of the NFL. But I'll make a mistake three or four or five times, and *then* I'll learn, which is the main thing.

Poor preparation can afflict anyone, from the rank and file to top management. In 1987 our team was supposed to defend a championship. We lost the first game in Chicago on Monday night, and then we missed a field goal at the end at home to lose to Dallas.

Then the strike hit, and our front office was caught by surprise; we weren't prepared to field a competitive team of replacements. Other teams had signed players they'd cut out of training camp, just in case they'd need people who already knew their system. We didn't do that. I wasn't too crazy about coaching a scab team, anyway, but now we had no shot. We lost those three "replacement" games by a combined score of 85–36. By the time the strike ended we were 0-5, with no margin for error, and we wound up at 6-9.

WELL-PREPARED LEADERS PLAN AHEAD FOR ALL CONTINGENCIES, INCLUDING THE ONES THEY CONSIDER UNLIKELY OR DISTASTEFUL.

Good preparation begins with organization. Before my staff meets with our players, we have to budget our time for the week, set our priorities. We decide which points we'll emphasize in depth, what we'll go through quickly, and what we'll skip altogether.

We usually follow a strict schedule. (Players are creatures of habit, and whenever we deviate we tell them ahead of time.) On Monday we review the old game and get the players to run and loosen up, to relieve some soreness and fatigue. Tuesday is the players' day off, but our staff works late to devise our new game plan. Then come our three major workdays, when the position coaches hold meetings in the morning and we all join for practice in the afternoon. On Wednesday and Thursday we stress basic running and passing plays, or defending against the opponents' basic blitzes. On Friday we move into more specialized parts of the offense: short-yardage, goal-line, red-zone passing, two-minute drills.

On Saturday we hold a special teams review and scouting report in the morning, and a final tape review of our opponent's offense and defense in the evening. Since we also may have to travel that day, it's just a light run-through—which means that Friday is a high-pressure day. At that point the players are torn between saving their bodies for the game and convincing the head coach that they're totally prepared. If they screw plays up on Friday, the coach is going to be unhappy, because he knows he's out of days.

But in truth, our practices are pressure-packed all week long. I believe that pressure is the only thing people respond to in any undertaking. Those who respond favorably will advance. Those who respond negatively are the drones, the tagalongs, the followers—and there's no room for them in the NFL. When a player deals successfully with pressure during the week, game pressure won't faze him.

For maximum value, practices must be challenging, both mentally and physically. They can't be passive. On Wednesday and Thursday we usually work out in full pads, at three-quarters speed. Our players receive a lot of technical information in the morning, and the only way you can be sure that they've absorbed it is by watching them execute that afternoon.

The pressure gets poured on heaviest in summer training camp. I might call out rapid-fire game situations; the players will run fifteen plays without a pause or huddle. Down the road, they won't have to wonder about my response in similar situations. They'll *know* what I want to do; all they'll have to do is execute.

Toward the end of the afternoon, we might run a two-minute drill. "Drew!" I'll call out to Bledsoe. "There's a minute-thirty to go, you got one time-out and you need 3 points. The ball's on your own 11 and the clock's running. Let's go!" If Drew's alert, he'll know he can't call his last time-out—he's got to spike the ball and waste a down instead.

Those drills are a proving ground. The heat takes its toll. Fatigue sets in on both coaches and players; tempers flare. We have a climate, in short, that is very much like the closing moments of a hard-fought game. Now I can gauge the players' conditioning, their discipline, their ability to function under adverse circumstances. Now I can see how they'll behave when it matters.

I tend to be more impatient during the week than at the game. I want those afternoon practices to be good all the time; it's a reflection of how good my teaching was that morning. I shoo the position coaches away from their units; the players need to do it on their own now. I don't tolerate imprecision, even on first run-throughs on Wednesday. I want my players to show it to me *today*.

To add to the pressure, I'll isolate players involved in key matchups. Say the Giants were preparing for Washington. After we'd been through the scouting report and all of our group work, I'd step into the huddle and say, "Brad Benson, if you don't block Dexter Manley on Sunday, and, Karl Nelson, if you don't block Charles Mann, it won't make any difference what the rest of you guys do, because we're going to get beat."

By Sunday our work should be finished. Before the game I'll limit my formal talking to logistics—"If we win the toss, let's take the ball"—and maybe a brief reminder or two. I don't like to disrupt players when the preparation's done. Too much eleventh-hour briefing is the mark of an insecure coach. It's better to leave people alone, let them get ready their own way. Their confidence will come not from a pep talk, but from the work they've done over the past six days.

PEOPLE PERFORM MOST RELIABLY WHEN THEY'RE SURE THEY CAN HANDLE THE TASK AT HAND—AND THAT SURENESS COMES ONLY WITH SPECIFIC PREPARATION.

At a financial transaction firm, the accounting department runs internal audits of every division in the company at six-week intervals, far more often than necessary. The routine can be time-consuming and monotonous . . . but when the IRS comes calling one year for a government audit, the people in accounting pass the test with ease because they know their job so well.

To out-prepare the other guy requires hard, steady work. More than that, it demands an understanding of how information is best imparted, how knowledge and technique are best retained.

SATISFY YOURSELF. As an assistant coach at West Point, I learned to be a perfectionist in practice. I'd stay out there with those players until every last movement was precise, until I got it the way I wanted it.

In the NFL you can't play the harsh taskmaster every day out; after a while, the Bataan approach loses impact. But there are times that you need to take a stern approach. When our Patriots have been underachieving, or we've been inefficient at practice earlier in the week, I'll lay down the hammer and turn the screws. "Fellas, this isn't going to be all that pleasant," I might tell my players, to set a businesslike tone. "I'm turning this clock off out here today, and when I like the way it looks, we're leaving. Until then, we're staying."

That's very disconcerting to the people on the field. Normally we practice from two-fifty to four-thirty. But once the clock's off, we might keep pushing it till five-thirty or even later. If we hit a snag, I'll stop everything and walk my players through it, as often as it takes. Along the way, we're making players accept the fact that they're all part and parcel of the problem. Rookies have a hard time with this—it's too much for their egos. They've been spoon-fed through college, they've coasted along on their considerable athletic skills, and sometimes they behave like they're still on scholarship. But I don't put up with that; I just keep pushing till they give me what the team needs.

WHEN LEADING A GROUP TOWARD AN IMPORTANT ACHIEVEMENT, DON'T COMPROMISE YOUR STANDARDS BASED ON PEOPLE'S COMPLAINTS OR CONVENTIONAL WORKLOADS. SETTLE FOR WHAT YOU WANT TO SETTLE FOR—AND WHAT SERVES THE GROUP'S BEST INTERESTS.

LESS IS MORE. At practice it's always tempting to say, "We'll run one more play." My position coaches always want to do more, because they don't want their people to look bad on Sunday. At some point I have to ask myself: "Am I running that play for me or for the team?"

You have to know when enough is enough. You have to respect people's limits, both mental and physical. We have about sixty basic plays in our offense. Our upcoming opponent probably runs another sixty. Now we're up to 120 potential practice "repetitions"—and that's not counting the three or four different defensive fronts that a Buddy Ryan might throw at you. We've got ten offensive linemen on the team, and five go at once, so an individual lineman would get about half of those repetitions.

That's nearly as much work as in a game—way too much for a daily practice. There are coaches who say,

"We'll just outwork 'em," but outworking them can be counterproductive. There's just so much tread on a tire, and you can't afford to wear it off before the flag comes down. So you have to choose your spots. You'll never be able to practice against all the multiple possibilities; some will have to get covered in the morning meetings and tape reviews. You're constantly balancing mental preparation against physical wear and tear. As the old saying goes, you want to work smarter, but not always harder.

Say you run an over-the-road freight business. You have a group of experienced, long-distance truck drivers, and it might seem more economical to schedule them for more miles at a stretch than to hire more guys. But people aren't machines, and you can't write off physical wear-and-tear as simple depreciation. Just one accident, and the lawsuits that might come out of it, can wipe out a lot of profit.

There has to be some flexibility in planning work-loads. When my team is coming off a tough Monday night road game, when it's worn down from travel and has a short week to recover, we may have lighter practices, without pads. I gauge what my players can handle, and that changes all the time.

The same philosophy applies to inserting new plays. A lot of coaches convince themselves that any good idea is practical, and that if it's practical it must therefore be *possible* for their team to execute. That can be a big mistake. A toss play might look terrific on paper, but the paper isn't playing against Reggie White. Our tight end has to block Reggie, and if he can't do it we might need a second man to help him—which means the play won't work as scripted.

When we audition a new play in our offense, I visualize how it should look *before* my players try it. If the reality doesn't match my mental picture, if I don't like how it looks on the field by Friday, I take it out. Some of my players and staff get frustrated at that; the more ammunition they have, the more comfort they feel. But coaches are in the discard business. We need to be sure about everything we're doing, to pick out what we need to win that week, and get rid of the rest. Sometimes you add by subtracting.

PREPARATION INVOLVES DIMINISHING RETURNS. YOU CAN'T TELL YOUR PEOPLE EVERYTHING YOU KNOW; YOU CAN'T TELL THEM VERY MUCH OF WHAT YOU KNOW; BUT WHAT YOU DO TELL THEM THEY BETTER GET.

ASSUME NOTHING. Coaches can't ever be afraid to repeat the most elementary fundamentals. As Tom Cahill used to tell my high school football team, *"First* who, *then* how. If you don't know who to hit, what am I teaching you how to hit him for?" Coach Cahill would get very dramatic at our first sign of confusion. He'd stop practice and point at each lineman, one at a time: "You have him, you have him, you have him. . . . You're running the ball here—now does everyone have it?" And then he'd go down the line *again*, repeating the matchups, and finally he'd say, "Now, goddamn it, *get* 'em!" Coach Cahill was adamant about the basics; they say you're a product of your environment, and there I am.

I emphasize the obvious all the time, especially with a younger team, because it's the obvious things that beat you if they're not taken care of. There are coaches who hold their players responsible for the entire play book, for knowing what to do even if the play hadn't been run all season. In my view, that's a good way to lose on principle. I'll go over things in practice that we ran last *week*; the players may groan, but they'll have no excuse for messing up.

THE ROAD TO EXECUTION IS PAVED BY REPETITION.

Every Friday we run a little special teams drill after practice that we call "Block That Kick." Before leaving the field, every member of our punt return team must run through in a simulated fashion and physically block a punt. You can't just take a leap and get the job done; you have to calculate the aiming point, three yards in front of the punter, and then you have to get your hands down in the right position. You have to perform the fundamentals.

This isn't exactly rocket science, and by the last weeks of the season it gets tedious for people, especially when we add on our weekly team drills on blocking extra points and field goals. But sooner or later, that exercise should pay off for us.

We're like the power company that stages unannounced emergency drills at least once a month. Everyone in the organization—from linemen to computer operators to substation supervisors—is held responsible for knowing where to be and what to do when the next brownout strikes. The same points may be covered in their employee manuals, but smart managers know that there's no way you can prepare yourself for *action* by leafing through a book.

BE A TEACHER, NOT A DRILL SERGEANT. The worst coach I ever encountered was an assistant one year at Wichita State. I was playing linebacker, and I was competent but not supremely gifted; there were games where I found myself in a physical stalemate, at best. But this coach had just one tune—it was always, "Hit him! Kill him!" He never gave me information I needed to combat my opponent; he was making me figure that out on my own.

I really resented that coach. When I went into this profession, I never wanted anyone to look at me like I used to look at him. So I might overcoach a player, might discuss things a little longer than necessary, but he'll know that I appreciate his problem, and that I'll do my best to help solve it.

To teach you have to listen as well as talk. When we experiment with something new in practice, our players' feedback is invaluable, especially from veterans who are honest about any problems they're having. (Rookies tend to say what they think the coach wants to hear.) If ten guys are functioning well but the one with the toughest task is uncomfortable, I've got to shore up that weak link before we try the play in a game. "Can we get this done?" I'll ask him. "How do *you* feel about it?" He might respond that he needs more work on it the next day. Or he might say he just doesn't feel good about it—and out the play goes.

RIDE YOUR BIG TALENTS HARDEST. The most skilled performers may sometimes coast along in practice, as if waiting for the "real" action on Sunday. When their coaches allow them to slide, these players become lost opportunities. Because it's the higher-level players that have the most room for improvement, and the greatest potential impact on a game's outcome. When a big talent is also well prepared, he can dominate; if he's lacking in preparation, he'll drift back to the pack.

Or as I'd tell Lawrence Taylor, who could be less than meticulous at practice, "If you don't know who to hit, you're just like everyone else."

IF 20 PERCENT OF THE PEOPLE ACCOUNT FOR 80 PERCENT OF AN ORGANIZATION'S ACHIEVEMENT, LEADERS NEED TO GIVE SPECIAL SUPPORT TO THOSE HIGH ACHIEVERS.

Harry Carson had been a Pro Bowl player in '78 and '79, but missed out the following year. When I joined the Giants as defensive coordinator in 1981, I could see that he'd picked up bad habits in technique and positioning. Despite Carson's stature, I wouldn't let either of us get complacent. I put in a lot of time prodding and challenging him, and Harry responded like an eager rookie. He raised his performance to a new level and became our most consistent defensive player. He made the Pro Bowl again that year—and for the next six years in a row.

As various forces—the salary cap, free agency, expansion —narrow the talent gap among NFL teams, the preparation gap will decide even more games than before. In the age of parity, a small edge in preparation can get parlayed into a decisive swing in the end result.

You see the same thing in business the world over. International computer networks have leveled the corporate playing field. With critical information now instantly routed wherever it's needed, it's harder for companies to dominate just because they're bigger or older than the competition, or because they've stockpiled a core of experts. Nowadays they better be *prepared* to compete if they want to protect their bottom line.

In my business, some tiny detail that you covered in training camp may deliver a key victory, which in turn gives your team impetus and confidence, and suddenly you have a snowball of success.

In our last game of the '94 season, the Patriots went to Soldier Field in Chicago to face a team in exactly the same position: We both needed a win to make the playoffs. We were struggling it out, leading 6–3 in the third quarter, when the Bears' Kevin Butler came in for a 38-yard field goal try. All season long we'd talked about blocking kicks, but we'd yet to produce one.

Until then. Troy Barnett, a first-year defensive end and special teams player who'd made only seven tackles all year, barreled through the line and smothered Butler and the ball.

We took our lead into halftime, and the Bears failed to score again; that block seemed to deflate them. We drove for a touchdown late to lock up the game and our playoff spot.

That was a great feeling, as good a feeling as I've ever had in football. In the locker room I stood up and told the players how proud I was: "No one fought harder than you guys. You were down and out, on the ropes and bleeding, but you didn't crack, and you stayed together."

A little later, as I sat on the bus after the game, I thought about how far we had come. This team really had depth of character; it had taught itself what it was. And yet the season's ending might have soured but for a little-used rookie. He was an unlikely hero who'd been prepared to make an unlikely play—thanks to those monotonous weekly drills in practice.

8.

RESOURCEFULNESS

THE BEST TEAM I EVER COACHED AGAINST WAS THE 1985 CHI-
cago Bears. The Bears' notorious defense had it all: quality
parts, a good philosophy, and, most of all, unshakable confidence. But people forget that Chicago was also the top-scoring
team in the league; they had a hard-nosed leader in Jim Mc-
Mahon, a tremendous runner in Walter Payton. And they had
a tough, seasoned, determined coach in Mike Ditka.

I knew the Bears were better than our Giants that year. If
we'd played them ten times, we might have beaten them twice.
But when we faced them in the conference semifinals, I honestly thought we had a chance.

On a cold, windy day in January, we lost the game, 21–0.

I was devastated by that loss, I really was. As I boarded
the bus to the airport, I thought about what lay ahead: another
off-season, another college draft, another pre-season and
training camp, another regular season and first-round playoff
game—just to get back where I'd been standing that day in

Chicago. And I frankly didn't know if we were capable of getting back there, if I'd ever get the same opportunity.

I said nothing to my team or staff after the game, and little to the media. I got off the bus, got on the plane, and sat there without a word. The team's owners, Tim and Wellington Mara, came up to console me: "Nice going, Bill, it was a great year, we'll get 'em next year." My general manager, George Young, said, "Gee, tough game, you did a great job this season."

And I just felt like the world had ended and everything decent had died.

Sitting next to me on that plane ride home was a seventy-year-old man named Mickey Corcoran, my high school basketball coach and a guy that I love. He'd stood behind me my whole career, came out most days to our Giants practices. You'd expect *this* guy to say something nice to me.

As I recall, we were somewhere over Pennsylvania, some three hours after the game, when Mickey tapped me on the side of the leg and piped up, "You know something, Parcells? You got to figure out a way to beat those goddamn guys."

I looked at him and said, "Hey, Mick, they're pretty good on defense, you know."

"They're *magnificent*," Mickey replied. "And you got to find a way to beat them."

That was like a pail of cold water—it cleared my head in a snap. Right there I started to focus on the next season. Right then I resolved to go forward, *to find a way to win.*

I knew I couldn't beat the Bears by myself. The very next day I met with my staff and said, "Fellas, I know they're all telling you we did pretty well this year. But in my mind we didn't do well enough. We're going to get it going, and we're going to win this thing next year."

Now I had my coaches thinking like me. At first they hadn't wanted to hear it—they were devastated, too. But when you set off on a quest, you need to enlist others; Columbus didn't sail that boat by himself. You have to foster collaboration. It gives you a surge of power when you have others with you, striving toward the same goal.

Our next step was to follow Mickey's directive—to figure out what we needed to do. A coach has to be honest with himself. If we played the Bears again and both teams stayed the same, I knew the outcome wouldn't change. To compete with them, we needed to get more dynamic on offense. The Bears were so aggressive that now and then they'd give you an opening for a big play—*if* you could survive the avalanche of their defense. That avalanche wasn't so deadly as long as you kept the game close; Buddy Ryan, Chicago's defensive coordinator, was far more aggressive with a lead. If you could somehow hold the Bears at bay, you might get them back on their heels.

The Giants *were* much improved in 1986. With Joe Morris, along with a better blocking fullback and a more experienced line, we now owned the best running game in the league. Mark Bavaro had developed into a threat at tight end. An influx of half a dozen draft choices made our defense deeper and more talented. Could we have beaten the Bears in the playoffs that season? We'll never know, because Washington knocked them off by exploiting the big play—the long pass—before our paths crossed.

But I do know this: The Bears wouldn't have shut us out that year. That Giants team could score under any conditions;

we weren't the same as the '85 edition. We were better because we'd been forced to become more resourceful—because an old coach reminded a younger coach that the test isn't over until you come up with an answer.

Successful organizations must be ready to adapt to new environments, no matter how well they've done in the past. Think of the small-town hardware store that built a loyal clientele by offering a broad array of items and strong customer service. Then a Home Depot outlet moves in two miles down the interstate—and that small-town store faces tougher competition in pricing and inventory than ever before.

The status quo won't be good enough anymore, that much is clear. And there's no way that the smaller store can match Home Depot across the board, item for item. So the store's manager devises a strategy that addresses the challenge at hand:

THE STAFF IS INSTRUCTED TO WORK EVEN HARDER ON ALERT SERVICE AND SPECIAL ORDERS, TO SHORE UP OLD CUSTOMERS' LOYALTY.

INVENTORY IS EXPANDED, AS SPACE ALLOWS, TO FEATURE UNCOMMON ITEMS THAT THE VOLUME-ORIENTED CHAIN OUTLET WON'T CARRY.

THE STORE CARVES OUT A SPECIAL AREA OF SUPERIORITY IN SHELVING MATERIALS OR HIGH-QUALITY HAMMERS OR SPECIALTY LIGHTING—WHATEVER MIGHT BEST GET A CUSTOMER IN THE DOOR AND OFF THE INTERSTATE.

REPEAT CUSTOMERS ARE OFFERED SPECIAL DISCOUNTS THROUGH DIRECT MAIL APPEALS AND OTHER TARGETED MARKETING.

THE STORE'S PRICING STRUCTURE IS RE-VAMPED TO BECOME AS COMPETITIVE AS POSSIBLE WITH THE CHAIN—AND EVEN TO UNDERCUT IT ON OCCASION WITH LIMITED, LOSS-LEADER SALES.

The strategic options are virtually endless, though not all of them will work. Trial and error is part of the process; it's rarely fatal to try something and fail. The greater danger lies in hiding behind tradition while the world keeps turning. Resourceful managers tinker and adapt until they find a winning formula.

There are games that unfold as if you'd scripted them. We implement our game plan and go in for a quick score. Then we stop them on defense and head in for another touchdown. It's like apple pie—we're just picking up a piece anytime we want to.

But there are many Sundays where nothing goes as planned. Your team isn't executing, or the other side has altered its defense to take something away from you, or the wind is gusting to fifty miles per hour. There is such a swirl of variables contained within football, so many games within the game, that what happens on the field may be in direct conflict with what you've prepared for. The score and clock alone often dictate a new strategy. Your script isn't so useful any-more; your choreography needs some drastic revision.

In such stressful circumstances, it's natural for teams to dissolve into infighting, chaos, exhaustion. The players' frus-tration is compounded by the physical beating they're taking. They're not sitting behind desks in air-conditioned rooms. They have to sort things out with one another when they can barely talk, because they're too busy trying to breathe. But that's precisely the time when a good team somehow regains its poise, and a strong coach helps it to change course and adjust.

Today's changing global economy has injected all-time high levels of stress into almost any business you can name. The modern business climate is stormy and unstable; the peo-ple inside it are buffeted by long hours, layoffs, and sometimes out-and-out chaos. They need strong direction to keep their equilibrium, and to feel confident in risking the changes the future will demand.

BY MAKING NEEDED ADJUSTMENTS, YOU HAND YOUR PEOPLE A POWERFUL EDGE. YOU CAN'T GUARANTEE THEIR SUCCESS; THEY DON'T SELL INSURANCE FOR THAT. BUT YOU'RE GIVING THEM THE BEST POSSIBLE CHANCE.

It's my senior year in high school, and we're losing a game by one point with twelve seconds left. We call time-out. Mickey Corcoran looks at me and says, "We're going to get you the ball on the left side of the lane, with your back to the basket, with about eight seconds left. Your job is to score with it."

Mickey can't tell me what to do with the ball once I get it; that will hinge on how the defense plays me. But he's created a reliable plan to get us an *opportunity* to score, and it works just like he drew it up—I hit the shot and we win. That game etched an indelible mark on me. To this day I try to do the same with my players: to help them anticipate situations as best as I can, and then hope I've instilled enough flexibility and confidence for them to adjust as they go.

There's nearly always a way to win if you can find it, but the steps may not be numbered like an Arthur Murray dance floor. You need people who understand what allows you to win and what causes you to lose. You need leaders who aren't bound by convention. A truly resourceful person won't always find the solution through some methodical, preconceived plan; there are times when sheer instinct leads you to your goal. Roger Staubach was like that when he quarterbacked the Cowboys. The game was never over when Roger had the ball, and you had no idea what he was about to do next.

Once I watched Bobby Knight's Indiana team play on the road against Michigan State. The Hoosiers were down one with forty-four seconds to go in the game, and this was before they had a shot clock. The book said you took the ball up the floor, ran the clock down to fifteen or twenty seconds, called a time-out, and set up a play. But Knight didn't go by the book. His team brought the ball up, held it till there was three seconds left—and then made the shot to win the game.

The next day I called my friend Bobby and said, "Tell me what you were thinking there."

And he said, "I'm thinking this: Inbounding the ball's a dangerous proposition in its own right. And I don't know that

I'm going to get a better shot by setting my offense, because it lets *them* set something up in their defense that I'm not prepared for. Taking it to the end allowed my team to function; I just thought it gave us a better chance to win."

This time Bobby had found a way by stepping back and letting his players make adjustments on their own. The key, of course, was that he'd prepared them for that eventuality in practice.

Resourceful coaches strive to have *more* ways to win than the other team. It's easier to be resourceful when you have more resources; great players give you more flexibility, more options to work with. But even when we lack star talent, we still try to generate extra chances for our players. Forcing more opposition turnovers (and eliminating our own), cutting down on penalties, refusing to give up big plays—all of these create more opportunities to score, and therefore to win.

As an industry gets more competitive, you have to pay attention to the *hidden* factors in success, to look beyond your obvious concerns in sales or service. Often that means getting involved with less glamorous components of your operation, like the warehouse serving a retail furniture outlet. A typical manager might sit in the showroom and skim through the warehouse reports—until six-thousand-dollar couches start falling off the trucks, and the whole business is disrupted.

But the resourceful manager will go the extra yard, making regular visits to the warehouse *before* a crisis develops. He'll get to know the workers there, see how the operation works at ground level. Even if the warehouse is making timely deliveries, with a low percentage of damaged goods, there might be room for improvement or greater efficiency, maybe a way to cut costs from ten dollars to five dollars per unit. When you multiply those savings by tens of thousands of units, you can see the potential for hidden profits behind those warehouse doors.

In football, as in any sport, a strong defense is the obvious way to gain a consistent edge over your opponent. But against the best teams, you can't afford to stop there. Often overlooked are all the *hidden* points created by your special teams, which execute 20 percent of the plays. Each of those plays determines either field position or points on the board; they sway the outcome significantly more than the average offensive or defensive play.

Punt protection, in particular, is one of the most critical and complex areas of the game. A strong punt with good downfield coverage can gain 50 yards of field position. A weak punt with ineffective coverage may gain only 10 yards. If you accept the premise that every 100 yards—no matter how you gain it—is eventually worth 7 points, the difference between the strong punt and the weak punt represents about 3 points.

When you consider that *25 percent* of the games in the NFL are decided by 3 points or less, that's a significant difference.

To take this a step further, the most dramatic turnaround play in football is a blocked punt. It swings points and momentum; it's a very strong deterrent to winning for the victim.

So it seems to me that if we put an accurate, strong-legged punter on the field, and surround him with both reliable protection and speedy, sure-tackling cover men, we have found a potential way to win—even in a game where our offense might be sputtering or our defense is neutralized. We've found a subtle but powerful way to gain an advantage.

Some other guidelines for the resourceful:

TARGET YOUR OPPONENTS WHERE THEY ARE STRONGEST. When we played San Francisco during my time with the Giants, we always wanted to knock Joe Montana off his feet early in the game, and the more often the better. We weren't looking to hurt Montana, but the guy was such a great player that he'd orchestrate his team right into the end zone unless you did something early to disrupt him.

The same principle applies to our selection of personnel. In our most recent draft in New England, a lot of people expected us to emphasize running backs or wide receivers, and were surprised when we chose two cornerbacks among our top four picks. Our reasoning was simple. When your top divisional rival is the Miami Dolphins, you better have quality tools to contain Dan Marino's downfield passing attack.

PLAY FROM YOUR STRENGTHS, BUT KEEP YOUR OPTIONS OPEN. Any decent game plan will stress what you do well, and thereby hide some of your weaknesses. When Japanese carmakers first entered the U.S. market, they didn't do battle with the Cadillac Fleetwood or Lincoln Continental; they found their wedge with economical compacts, the cars they did best.

At the same time, it's dangerous to become too reliant on any one element. I think that's what happened to Don Coryell's aerial circus acts in St. Louis and San Diego. These teams had some success, and they were highly entertaining; they even had their own special identity, "Air Coryell." Their pass-happy style was good for television, good for the league—good for everybody but the teams themselves. They never achieved at the highest level. When San Diego faced a team like the Oakland Raiders, whose man-to-man defense could disrupt at least one or two wide receivers, the Chargers were dead. They had no contingency plan to fall back upon, no other ways to win.

I think the same thing has happened to John Elway in Denver—and some people might call me a hypocrite, since my own Drew Bledsoe threw more passes last season than any quarterback in NFL history. But we're going to be changing that, and soon. While we need to exploit Bledsoe's talent, our goal is to have a productive, efficient, well-rounded unit, a team that's balanced in its attitude. Any single player or element can be negated by injury, lackluster execution, an opponent's adjustment, even the weather. A balanced team is able to shift gears and find another avenue of attack.

TAKE THE FIRST OPENING THAT PRESENTS IT-SELF, BUT STAY AMBITIOUS FOR SOMETHING BETTER. You don't know how the other team's defense will operate till the game starts. If you have a powerful, multifaceted offense, they'll usually "give" you something they think they can concede without too much damage—short swing passes to your halfback, for example. If you settle for those crumbs throughout the game, you might find yourself neutralized and left holding a consolation prize. To win most games, you have to devise a way to do what *you* want to do.

But until you figure that out and identify other options for your quarterback, you need to take what's available. Blind attacks can backfire. So you take what you can, probe the holes in their defense, and solve the problem as you go.

Like losing teams, unprofitable companies have a special need for resourcefulness. When the economy takes a downturn and you're suddenly operating at a loss, it's human nature to retreat, to turn conservative, to lock up your remaining assets rather than attack your problems with new initiatives. In the worst case, short-term panic can lead to long-term paralysis, to a stagnant operation that writes its own death sentence.

Resourceful leaders get even more imaginative when they're at a disadvantage. They know that a crisis calls for a higher level of problem-solving, and that solutions are no longer luxuries, but necessities. They buck up their troops and treat crisis as a white-water adventure—as something the organization will have to use all of its tools and collective ingenuity to get through.

In the NFL it's not unusual to find yourself up against a team with more talent. At those times I hope that we can hold our own in certain critical areas, and somehow eke out a win with a gamble, a trick, the element of surprise. Even a temporary, situational edge can pay big dividends for the team's confidence. If you select the right plays to reel off three first downs to begin the game, your offense starts thinking, *Gee, we can move the ball against these guys.*

When the Patriots played San Diego in 1994, the Chargers were 8-2 and en route to the Super Bowl. We were 4-6, fresh off our overtime victory over Minnesota, but still hanging by our fingernails. What's worse, San Diego had established itself as a power running team with Natrone Means, and we'd already shown a weakness in dealing with that kind of attack, since we weren't overly big or physical on defense.

What we had going for us was a two-pronged plan. The first prong was to force San Diego to run outside—we didn't think Means had the speed to get out there and turn the corner. The second prong was to put double coverage on Ronnie Harmon, their third-down, chain-moving guy. We were determined that Harmon would not beat us.

Our plan was on the money that day. Means never got untracked, and Harmon caught just one pass all game, for ten yards. Our defensive stands allowed our offense to get us a 10–0 lead at the half, and by then our team was starting to believe they could put these guys away. That quick start gave us the confidence to attempt the undertaking, to fight harder and go on.

You can't devise resourceful strategies unless your staff has the proper outlook. There are always problems on a football team, as in any other business. And there are coaches, and managers, who can sit around indefinitely expounding upon those problems. *Those people will not help you find a way to win.* When a football team has lost three straight, or a company's earnings have slumped for three consecutive quarters, it's no news that something's wrong. The challenge is to identify exactly what the problem is, and then to solve it. That second part, the action step, is what separates leaders from analysts.

THE ABILITY TO RECOGNIZE A PROBLEM IS USELESS UNLESS YOU ARE ALSO ABLE TO FIX IT.

Let's say that I'm watching a tape before the college draft, and I see a wide receiver drop a catchable pass. "He wasn't concentrating," my scout might tell me. Or: "He didn't look the ball into his hands." Either or both may be true, but it makes no difference unless I'm sure we can correct the weakness.

I have a coach on my Patriots staff whom I like very much. When we worked together in New York, he was instrumental in developing several highly productive players. Then he went to work for a losing franchise, and spent a lot of time around people who'd been beaten down. When I brought him to New England he wasn't quite the same guy. The players on his unit—and we've shuffled the deck more than once—are never quite good enough for him. The glass is stuck at half-empty. He's like the manager who always needs just one more sales rep to cover the territory: "It's not *our* fault that we can't do the job—we just don't have the resources."

Once this kind of attitude infiltrates your system, it's insidious; people pick it up by osmosis. A leader has to stop it in a hurry. You have to say, "Well, boys, this is what we're going to do now, and it's time to do it. Don't get all hot and sweaty telling me why things are the way they are. It's time to find the solution. It's time to *do* something."

The fact is, they're not going to cancel the season just because the New England Patriots have yet to collect twenty-two perfect prototype players. We've got to play sixteen games, and our owner won't much like it if we forfeit. We'll bring in the best people we can, and then I want to hear my staff say, "We'll just play this guy and get it done with him."

I understand that players have different capabilities. Sometimes you have to gear or alter the job to fit the individual—that's where your creativity comes into play. When you ask people to perform tasks that they find impossible, you're failing them as a leader, no matter how philosophically sound those tasks may be in the abstract. You're also tolerating defeat, with a built-in alibi: "We just don't have enough talent, so we're going to fail."

When the Giants lost Phil Simms fourteen games into the 1990 season, a lot of doubt crept into our team. The experts noted that no one had ever won a Super Bowl with a backup quarterback. We'd clinched our division, we'd dominated most of the year, and now we were instant underdogs.

But I didn't have time for doubts or anxiety. As soon as Phil's injury happened, it was a challenge, a puzzle to be solved. We had to tailor our game plan to Jeff Hostetler's talents, then test it in our last two regular-season games. We won both in shaky fashion, and I could tell the team was jittery, but I also could see that we were adapting to our modified plan.

AT ITS MOST BASIC, RESOURCEFULNESS IS SIMPLY RESILIENCE—A REFUSAL TO QUIT OR GIVE IN, EVEN WHEN ALL SEEMS BLEAK.

For all its success in the regular season, that 1990 Giants team proved its mettle in the playoffs. After steamrolling Chicago, we traveled to San Francisco to play for the conference championship—one of the top two or three games I've ever been involved in. The 49ers had won two straight Super Bowls, and were being touted as the best team of all time if they could "threepeat." They'd already beaten us *with* Phil Simms earlier that year.

Hostetler played well that day, but Matt Bahr missed a field goal and old reliable Maurice Carthon dropped a very open touchdown pass. (We called him "Allstate" for some time after that.) With just over two minutes left, San Francisco had a 1-point lead and the ball in our territory . . . when we capitalized on a key mistake. Erik Howard jolted Roger Craig into a fumble, and Lawrence Taylor recovered it. Hostetler connected on two clutch passes before Bahr kicked a game-winning field goal with no time on the clock.

From there we advanced to our Super Bowl match against Buffalo, a team that had averaged 35 points a game, a team that was considered unstoppable. Needless to say, we were underdogs once again. The Bills had "the offense of the nineties"; we had the offense of the seventies. It was the Thoroughbreds against the slugs, the high techs versus the Neanderthals.

Hostetler took a tremendous pounding in the first half of that game, but he picked himself up to lead two long, game-

changing drives that bracketed halftime, and finished with his
best passing game ever. It's true that we needed to withstand a
field goal attempt by Scott Norwood at the very end, but we'd
deserved to win that game. We'd controlled the clock for more
than forty minutes, a Super Bowl record, and our defense had
dug in all day. Norwood's last kick was from 47 yards out, on
grass—not a high-percentage play.

The Neanderthals had done it. We had found a way to
win.

In bouncing back from adversity, or in staying a difficult
course, an organization can't count on spontaneity. It needs to
draw on stores of confidence and shared experience, of ingrained values.

Ten games into the '86 season, the Giants were 8-2. We'd
just beaten the Redskins, the Eagles, and the Cowboys in consecutive weeks—and we hadn't really achieved a thing. We
were tied with Washington in the standings, and Dallas was
still in it. Four of our last six games were away, beginning with
that tough road game with Minnesota.

In my state of the union, I told my team, "The race starts
here. Put all those wins behind you, because the race actually
starts here and now." Which somewhat offended my players,
because they'd just beaten their three big division rivals, and I
was throwing that away.

And then I told them, "We're like the pioneers. We've just
crossed the Plains, but that doesn't mean much now. Because
the whole league has reached the edge of the Rockies, and
most of these teams are going to fall by the wayside. The rock

slides will get some of them, the Indians will get some others, the floods and the grizzly bears will get a few more. A lot of teams will give in to the elements. But some of them are going to get through, and it might as well be us."

That might sound like a pretty corny speech, but I'd gotten my point across. As our players kept advancing, and clinched our division, and then home-field advantage for the playoffs, the players would talk about it: "Well, we got through; we're through the Rockies."

When the mountain seems steepest, leaders must provide more than tactical nuts and bolts. To instill a resourceful mind-set throughout the organization, they have to try to *inspire* people, as well—to lay out the common agenda and goals in a way that will push others to see them through.

Our team's resilience started with our quarterback. Phil Simms had good skills, but what made him special was his toughness; in that category he ranked in the top one or two. He took some terrible physical beatings, especially from the Eagles under Buddy Ryan. When we brought defensive tackle Michael Pitts to New England from Philadelphia, the first thing he told me was how much his unit respected Phil Simms: "No matter what you did, he'd get up and come back at you. You couldn't knock him out."

The more difficult the game, the more hits he absorbed, the tougher Phil got. He'd rarely mutter a word about it; he'd just go on to the next play with that I'll-show-you look on his face. And a defense couldn't hurry him into a panicked, ill-conceived pass. If anything, Phil would stand too long in the pocket, unwilling to release the ball till he felt sure. That meant we had to hold the protection longer, and I can't count the times that Phil was hit late, just after a pass was thrown. His caution could exasperate me, but it also was the habit of a brave man.

I don't think you go too far without leaders like that. There are people in the business world who are totally non-competitive. Challenge them and they retreat. Place an obstacle in their path and they'll detour 28 miles in the other direction to avoid it.

These people get sorted out most quickly when the going gets roughest. It takes a rare strength to hold your spirit intact and keep from quitting too soon. It takes a strong group to forge on with full effort even when a contest seems temporarily out of control. Resourceful teams regroup to stem the tide, and adjust to get back into the game. They've got a fail-safe mechanism—they have the mental toughness to say, "Okay, we're down 13 points, but we're coming back."

In 1986 the Giants were trailing 17–0 in a Monday night road game in San Francisco. The 49ers had Montana in his prime, a wild crowd, and a taste for revenge, since we'd knocked them out of the playoffs the year before. At halftime I delivered my usual set piece: "Look, fellas, there's still time to win this game." That's all I said, and that's all I had to say, because this was a team that believed it. And then we told Simms, "We're going for their throat—we're going to open this up now."

We came out in the third quarter and *bang*, we got a quick score; *bang*, we got another one; *bang*, we got another one, and with six minutes left in the quarter we're ahead. In the fourth quarter San Francisco was driving for the winning touchdown, but we made the play at the end to beat them—a blitz by Andy Headen up the middle, on fourth down, that forced Montana to throw incomplete. We showed all kinds of resourcefulness that day: the capacity to take a beating, like a boxer who's been rocked and is way behind on points, but refuses to go down for the count; the ability to adjust and roar back, to reclaim momentum; and, finally, the will and instinct to make a play at the critical moment, to *do* something that guarantees the outcome.

Weaker teams can't do that. They crack, they relent, and their opponent moves in for the kill. They can't adjust till after they see the game tapes on Monday. But tomorrow's a day late in this game. In the red-white-and-blue world of the New England Patriots, Monday is a very bad day to solve problems.

When I came to New England in 1993, our players didn't even want to be known as Patriots. The veterans would almost conceal their identity outside the stadium, and the rookies soon found that they were lumped in with the failures of the past. It was a long, slow process to build a prideful foundation for this team, but we had to do it, because a team needs that pride to prop it up when things go badly on the field.

In our first game that season, we stayed close to Buffalo into the fourth quarter. But our team was playing scared—I could just *smell* it—and we were ready to crack. When the Bills cranked it up a notch, we started missing tackles and giving up on blocks; we just quit, and got blown out by 24 points. In our second game we got to overtime, where we're done in by a holding penalty and two panicked incompletions by Bledsoe. In our third game we came back and had a chance to send it into overtime, but our field goal try hit the middle of the crossbar and bounced back.

Through it all I can see that my team *wants* to win. They're looking for direction, but they lack the resolve, the commitment, the will within themselves; the results have been so bad for so long that they're not prepared to fight.

By the following year, though, it's different. My team is a little more confident, a little more poised. Then we make some mistakes, get shaken by a couple injuries, let down on defense —and suddenly we're 3-6, and the season is just about slipping away. As usual, the reporters are premature; in this business, you ascend to the throne too quickly, and fall to the depths just as fast. At my press conference, a beat writer asks: "Coach, how does it feel to be playing out the string?"

"We're not playing out the string," I reply. They all look at me and I know they're all thinking, *This guy isn't telling the truth—deep down inside, he knows.*

"What do you mean?" the beat writer says.

"Lookit, we are not eliminated from our goal, which is to improve our team over last year. Until I know we can't do that, we're not playing out the string. We're trying to win on Sunday and get to 4-6."

I really believed that; I thought our team was capable of doing better and making some strides. And the team read my response, and maybe it got them thinking, too. When we made our big second-half comeback against Minnesota that Sunday with our two-minute offense, a lot of elements had to fall into place for us. But none of it would have worked if we hadn't been ready to seize the opportunity—if we hadn't kept the faith.

With a winning team, you just have to show them where the next mountain is. With a losing team, when you've got the whole Rockies in front of you, and you haven't even scaled the first foothill, *that's* when a leader needs to be tough and resilient. While everyone around you looks back at past failures, you must lock your eyes forward, to the future. When your ship is being tossed in the storm, you have to keep an even keel.

For me it goes back to when I was five years old, to my first day on my own at the neighborhood playground in Hasbrouck Heights, New Jersey. It isn't long before I get into a little skirmish with a kid named Danny Astrella. He's older than me, maybe seven or eight. He's bigger than me. And as the last of fourteen children, a kid who grew up hard, he's *definitely* tougher than me. So I get pummeled. I try to fight back, but I can't fight him—he's too much.

So I go home bleeding from my first day on the playground. My mother's upset, but my dad just looks at me and says, "You all right?"

"Yeah."

And my dad says, "You got to go back out there tomorrow."

Well, that's the last thing I was expecting to hear. "I don't want to go back—he's going to beat me up again."

"You got to go," my dad insists, "because if you don't go tomorrow, you'll never be able to go. You got to sort this out. You're not looking for any trouble, but if trouble comes your way, you have to learn to deal with it."

So the next day I walk back to the playground, and Danny's out there . . . and nothing happens. It's all over; everything's fine. And Danny Astrella becomes my lifelong friend.

We all get beaten up in life. It's happened to me many times: when I took my first head coaching job at the Air Force Academy, and found myself stuck in a losing program; when I resigned my first NFL job, as linebacker coach with the Giants, to sell real estate and ease the pressure at home; when my first championship team never got a fair chance to defend its title, thanks to the '87 strike; when heart surgery forced me out of coaching for two years; when it seemed like those '93 Patriots would never win another game.

And each time, I vividly heard my father's voice. *You got to go back out there.* Each time it challenged me to get my butt in gear and *do* something, instead of quitting and pouting around.

You got to go back out there. Without that steadfast resilience, no leader or organization can survive at the top.

9

HUMILITY

BACK IN THE MID-SEVENTIES, WHEN I WAS COACHING DEFENSE AT Texas Tech in Lubbock, I noticed a middle-aged guy coming out to watch our spring practices. I didn't know who the man was, but I could tell he was all-Texan, down to the heavy drawl and leathery face. He wore a brown jacket with a gray border and a "B" on its breast. And every now and then he'd lean toward me and ask a question about what we were doing.

We had twenty practices that spring, and this guy must have made a dozen of them. At one of the last ones he said to me, "You know, you're a pretty good coach."

It was only later on that I found out what high praise I'd received. That guy in the brown jacket was Gordon Wood of Brownwood High School, then well on his way to winning four hundred-plus games. As far as I know, that's more than any other football coach has won in the history of the sport. Wood was a legend, and I was a nobody, but he made the five-hour round trip to Lubbock in the hope of picking up something new from me. The fire still burned; he was still striving to get better.

That's humility, and it made Gordon Wood quite an exception to the rule of human nature. Climbing to the top can be an ordeal, full of setbacks and adversity. But to get to the pinnacle and stay there is more difficult still. It goes back to the psychology of results; once a goal is reached, it takes rare maturity to avoid a letdown. Complacency sets in. Hunger dulls. Egos swell.

When the Patriots played Minnesota last year, we couldn't have made our spectacular comeback without a little help from the opposition. While the Vikings had the best record in the NFL at the time, they hadn't really achieved anything yet. But in my Wednesday pre-game conference call with the Minnesota media, I was getting questions like, "Coach, do you think the Vikings compare favorably to your Giants Super Bowl teams?"

Right there I knew that the players in Minnesota were in trouble—they were hearing things not conducive to success. Their local press had the team ascending to the throne, even though it had yet to reach the palace. I wasn't too surprised when the Vikings lost four of their last seven games, and were routed in the first round of the playoffs.

You see this all the time in pro sports. A team makes the playoffs and gets an impressive win, and the next week they're so self-satisfied that they barely show up. After the Cleveland Browns beat us in the first round last season, they went on to Pittsburgh and lost by 20 points. They were a good team, but they couldn't sustain it.

YOU'RE NOT TRULY SUCCESSFUL UNTIL YOU'RE CHALLENGED AT THE TOP LEVEL OF YOUR ABILITY—AND YOU CONSISTENTLY MARSHAL YOUR BEST EFFORT.

The backlash hits hardest after an organization achieves real greatness. (Ask the folks at IBM.) It's so hard to stay great after you win a championship. The media works overtime to find chinks in your armor. Every foe now makes you enemy number one; you've got what they want, and they'll do everything they can to seize it from you.

But the main threats, the ones that tear you down, are all internal: complacency, distraction, all the petty jealousies that come with the distribution of credit. You've all just been through the fight of your life, and now you have to jump right back into the ring, and your spirit isn't quite the same. The forces pulling you apart become a hell of a lot stronger than the ones that once held you together. In my book, any team that wins two championships in a row is just about a dynasty these days—that's how difficult it is to defend a title.

Our '87 Giants were a textbook case. When you win in New York, the town revels in a big way, and it's easy to get caught up in it. Everybody's got a little extra money in their pocket. Now we have a couple executives of the year, and I'm coach of the year, and everyone on the payroll is suddenly a quotable authority on how to build a championship team. A bunch of players write books, and I write one, too—I'm right in there with them. I'm under contract, but I get into a flirtation with the Atlanta Falcons, who are seeking a new head coach; I'm enjoying my new leverage, and maybe I'm still smarting over how the front office almost fired me back in 1983.

I could see from the start of training camp that we weren't as good as the year before. Some guys weren't quite as sharp; others were showing their age. A few, as I've noted, became greedy and demanding—they were riding the coattails of success, trying to cash in. While most of our players would regain their equilibrium, and with it their drive to be great again, it wasn't going to happen that year. There were some people in the organization who blamed our collapse on the strike, but that was just a convenient alibi. In truth, we weren't collectively mature or humble enough to *overcome* our prior success.

At one point I remember telling George Young, our general manager, that we ought to bus in the local schoolchildren to look at our operation—that it would make a perfect lesson about the downfall of the Roman Empire.

So I saw the decadence coming early on, but I didn't really *do* anything about it, and I didn't get much help from upstairs. The whole organization fell down. Our management tumbled into the post-Super Bowl trap. They got a little smug and comfortable—they presumed that their presence alone would suffice to maintain excellence. The voice from the arena, my voice, was as loud as ever, but the ears weren't hearing as well. When I pointed to deficiencies in our personnel, the response was, "Well, that's just how Bill is, he's never satisfied."

It's as if they were telling me: If it ain't broke, you don't fix it. But something's *always* breaking on a football team, either minor or major. It's like a high-performance car with an old muffler. If you don't replace the part when it starts to get noisy, at some point the whole car slows down.

IN A COMPETITIVE ENVIRONMENT, TO REMAIN THE SAME IS TO REGRESS.

Any business that markets computer software, for example, knows the learning curve is so steep that constant updates and improvements are necessary. You might have developed the best word-processing program anyone's ever seen, but if you sit back to read your press notices, someone will create a better one.

Not every winner falls victim to complacency. Don Shula does an amazing job, year after year, of staying impervious to the side effects of success. But more typical is the college basketball coach who makes a big splash in the NCAA tournament—and the next year he's recruiting these rat kids to his school, and half of them are being bought, and they're cutting class and into drugs. . . . There's a slippery slope out there, and the higher you get, the steeper the slide.

In recent years no franchise has suffered more from the distribution of credit than the Dallas Cowboys. The stage was set by two tremendously powerful, big-ego guys: Jerry Jones and Jimmy Johnson. Now, Jones has done an outstanding job since he bought the team—developing apparel sales, enhancing the team's image, moving it up-market. He also was smart enough to hire Johnson, who happens to be one of the soundest, best-prepared coaches in the country.

But after Johnson led Dallas to two straight championships, to much deserved acclaim, the relationship fell apart in a public open-field battle. Soon Johnson was out—driven out, it seemed to me, by jealousy in upper management. They found a solid guy to replace him, but the turmoil took its toll; the Cowboys slipped a bit last season, and they're in danger of slipping some more.

I think it all could have been avoided if Jerry Jones had understood his role—and his limits—within the organization. In the NFL, there's only one product that matters: a team's on-field performance. The head coach is a major ingredient in that product, and the really good ones don't come a dime a dozen. An owner can be the greatest marketing whiz in the Western world, but when that on-field product declines, it eventually drags everything else down with it.

It's common for the big boss to overrate his importance— who's going to tell him he's wrong? The higher the level of management, the harder it can be for individuals to separate their own interests from those of the organization. But football teams don't need owners who patrol the sidelines on Sunday, drawing attention to themselves. They need owners who hire competent professionals, give them support, and then step to the side and let them work.

In pro sports today, humility is an endangered virtue, especially among young players who've received so much, so soon. I now live in Massachusetts, and the adulation being heaped upon Drew Bledsoe in this part of the country makes my head spin. He's just twenty-three years old, and his team has yet to win a playoff game, but he's been declared an instant hero. If you were to swallow the hype, Bledsoe has already joined the select circle of Boston superstars; he's taken his place alongside Ted Williams, Bobby Orr, Bill Russell, and Larry Bird.

I'm not arguing about Bledsoe's talent here. He's got every tool you'd want in a passer: range, accuracy, touch, vision, the quick release. Drew's very imposing physically—he's 6-5, and I expect he'll fill out to 250 pounds—and he's pretty tough. But he's just 20 percent around the circle, just learning to find his way. It's my job to make sure he keeps his *to be* mentality amid all the distractions and easy admiration. As talented as Bledsoe may be, he's not talented enough to get to the highest level without an airtight dedication to his craft.

As I've told Drew many times, I don't want a celebrity quarterback. I want a guy who gets his team in the end zone and wins games, and most of all the big games. I want my quarterback to be proud of his team's achievement, not vain about his passing stats. A couple decades from now, Terry Bradshaw will be a bigger name in football history than John Elway, because Bradshaw helped win some Super Bowls. But twenty-three-year-olds don't leave the factory equipped with historical perspective; some of that has to be installed by the coach.

I have similar concerns about Ben Coates, who broke the all-time reception record for tight ends last year, in his fourth season in the league. When something like that happens, a coach has to consider what the player is hearing when he's not around you—"Aw, Ben, you're the best tight end in football" —and how success may affect him.

Coates is an honest player, and he's demonstrated a strong work ethic in the past, but *any* player is vulnerable to slippage when he figures he's proven himself. It's easy to forget the journey that got him where he is, and to start looking at less distant horizons. This past winter, I got worried when Coates told me, "The year I had was just so fortunate, I don't know whether I could ever have another one like it."

"Why not?" I replied. "Did you ever think you might have a *better* one?"

After an organization breaks through to a new level, its leaders have to guard against the Genius Syndrome—the notion that they must be *the* reason for success. NFL coaches aren't immune, but they're less vulnerable than most. A coach is trained to look forward, rather than bask in the past, if only because he's the first person to be scrutinized; he's the guy with the target on his chest. He gets the big head at his peril.

Take Jerry Glanville. He was a very good football coach— he knew what it took to win—but he had this need to be *the show*, to promote himself above his team. He'd drive a motorcycle onto the field for a Monday night football game, decked out in a black cowboy hat and sunglasses, and the Mardi Gras didn't stop at kickoff. Glanville regarded the run-and-shoot offense as his trademark, and he turned his team into a carnival—seals to the left, trapeze guys to the right.

In the late eighties I thought Glanville's Houston Oilers had the best personnel in the league by far, but they never made it to a conference championship game. In the end his teams were always dangerous but never consistent.

Wherever gimmicks replace content, the product suffers. I happen to like Marv Albert's play-by-play work in basketball, with his signature "Yes!" to punctuate a score. But when a TV guy goes overboard—when Dick Vitale starts screaming about *his* "Diaper Dandies" and "Prime-Time Players"—the shtick gets bigger than the game, and the game shrinks.

Remember New Coke? The board of egos at the Coca-Cola Company figured they could expand their market share by slapping a new name and label on a can, and backing it with a catchy ad campaign. How could they fail? They ruled the beverage world; if they put the stuff out, people were sure to drink it.

They figured wrong, and New Coke has just about disappeared from your local supermarket shelves.

When I got sick and left coaching for two years, I found out that I wasn't irreplaceable, after all. I was suddenly a nonfactor, a peripheral figure, and I realized that I'd been a cog in the assembly line all along. But there are coaches and players—and managers in any business you can name—who think they *are* the assembly line, and that's where their troubles start.

While complacency and arrogance are insidious diseases, there are steps you can take to inoculate your organization and keep it humble:

TRAIN THE SPOTLIGHT ON THE GROUP, NOT THE INDIVIDUAL. Players are ultimately judged by how many games their team wins, not by their sack totals or completion averages. Sales managers are eventually rated by their divisions' productivity, not their individual figures. That long-term reality, however, often clashes with a company's short-term, hero-building style. Praise and attention—and, in some cases, incentives—should focus more on collective success, less on one person's accomplishment.

PLACE ACHIEVEMENTS IN PERSPECTIVE. In our first game of the '94 season, Drew Bledsoe threw for 421 yards, far surpassing any other game he'd had as a pro. With everyone buzzing about this tremendous performance, I had to remind Drew that he'd also forced four balls into interception territory, that two of them had been picked off, and that those plays had probably kept us from winning.

It goes back to my high school basketball days under Mickey Corcoran. "You can score 20 points," he'd tell me, "but if your guy gets 22, what good are you?"

When people are riding high, a leader needs to function as a reality check, as the honest adviser, to keep them at an even keel. In 1986 the Giants had the toughest, most consistent blocking line in the business—it had gotten to the point where these offensive linemen were making little names for themselves. But late in the regular season, Joe Morris was held to only 14 yards in our narrow win over San Francisco. For a while after that I called our line "Club 14"—just a small, sarcastic reminder that people who rest on their laurels are soon lying flat on their backs.

KEEP SETTING NEW GOALS. About ten minutes after we won our first Super Bowl in '86, I was called to a TV interview with Brent Musberger. And Musberger's first question was, "So, Bill, do you think you can repeat next year?" I wanted to whack the guy in the mouth; he'd stolen the joy of our celebration, and you don't get many of them in our game.

But maybe Musberger did me a favor, because right away I knew I wanted to win one more championship, just so everybody would know it wasn't an accident. In reality, no one gets lucky and wins a Super Bowl; I know that for a fact. But now I had something more to prove, and I drove myself hard as ever till we won the second one four years later.

There's a rodeo bull rider I follow named Tuff Hedeman. He's won three world championships in his sport, which is very difficult to do; he's the Joe Montana of bull riders. After he won his third one, Tuff didn't rest his bull rope to party or go to Disney World or hit the talk-show circuit. He just moved his gear on to Denver, where the title hunt would start all over again—and, as Tuff said, "The bull won't care what I did last week."

MEASURE EXCELLENCE BY PERFORMANCE, NOT REPUTATION. We all know people who trade on past achievements to coast along in the present. (The NFL is full of them.) A leader needs to do battle with these coun- terfeit performers; if allowed to slide by, they'll make the organization flabby, inefficient, stagnant. You have to demonstrate that you can't be fooled, that *you know what's going on*—whether you do it with game tapes, performance reviews, or internal audits.

In my business, humility is best maintained when

both coach and player know exactly what transpired on the field, good or bad. A lot of athletes are overrated by those outside this little loop of reality. But you can't let a player hide behind his agent's perception, or the media's perception, or the fans' perception, or even the front office's perception. You can't have any secrets, or leave uncomfortable things unsaid. You have to toss out the rose-colored glasses and zero in on the truth.

To do less will jeopardize both parties, even when you're at the crest of success. Championships are momentary things; they buy some time, but not security. When you win, you get to stay a little while longer; when you lose, you get to go. If Tom Landry can get fired, anybody can get fired; if Phil Simms can get released, no player is safe. The instant you relax, or drop off, or rely on *who* you are rather than *what* you're doing, you're on the express lane to the chopping block.

SUCCESS IS NEVER FINAL, BUT FAILURE CAN BE.

RESPECT YOUR MENTORS. We all need a sounding board once in a while, no matter how much we've accomplished. In my early years in the NFL one of my main influences was Chuck Knox, the long-time head coach with the Rams, Bills, and Seahawks. Chuck was the consummate football man; his whole identity was wrapped up in his profession. Of all the veteran coaches in the league at that time, he was also the most willing to help a younger colleague. I could ask him about anything, from game strategies to how to approach my next contract, and he'd share his wisdom every time. After I'd been in New York a few years, he'd call me up and ask *my* opinion; he never assumed he knew it all.

I'm fortunate to have another mentor in Al Davis, the Raiders' managing partner. Al has taught me a lot—most of all, that you cannot stop striving for greater things. The search to improve never ends. Al may have a checkered reputation in some quarters in this league, but he's been a loyal friend to me, a smart guy I could always trust. A lot of years ago I think he sensed that we were kindred spirits, that I shared his passion for our game.

WHEN CHOOSING AN ALLY, IGNORE POPULAR OPINION. GO BY YOUR DIRECT EXPERIENCE WITH THE PERSON INSTEAD.

If I'm famous for anything, it's probably for getting wet in public—for being on the business end of a Gatorade shower. It started when I coached the Giants, with practical jokers like Harry Carson and Lawrence Taylor. It carried over to New England last season when we beat Buffalo, with Bledsoe and Coates leading the perpetrators. In 1986, when we won so many games in a row, our home fans would egg the players on to get me. It became a part of Americana—as I traveled through airports, people would approach me and say, "Hey, Bill, watch out for the bucket!"

For all that, you'd be surprised at how many people resented the stunt—they thought it took away from the dignity of the profession. They said, "You don't ever see them doing that to Don Shula or Tom Landry." Well, that's true—but I'm not either one of those guys.

A big part of humility is not taking yourself too seriously. When you live with your players eleven hours a day, six days a week, twenty-four weeks or more out of the year, you can't rehearse your personality. You can't be putting on a face, or they'll see right through you.

Leaders have to be themselves. Some coaches like to fraternize with their players; others stay up in the tower. Some guys are distant and technical, others harsh and abrupt, others warm and emotional. But none of that makes any difference as long as you get results and your team functions on Sunday.

I've always appreciated a good joke, even when I'm the butt of it. If you can't laugh at yourself in the NFL, the job gets pretty dry. Because most of the time it's push-push-push. And the more you push our players, the more success you have; and the more you want to go forward and the harder you push. You've got to let them breathe once in a while.

With the Gatorade my players have always had good timing. They wait until there's a minute or less to go, when my headset's off and they know I'm not working anymore. I think those showers reflect something positive about our relationship —that they're glad I'm in there with them. That they're thanking me, almost.

I've always spent time talking to my players, getting to know them. I try to say something to each individual every day—not a long dialogue, just, "How you feeling? You looked good in the tapes last night, keep goin'." On the field I may use last names, but in the locker room or my office, I stick to first names. And even now, when I'm old enough to be their father, they can always call me Bill; I never thought that you got respect from a certain mode of address.

I don't socialize with my players, but I like to meet their wives and see their babies. I care about whether they're paying their taxes, or if their child is over the chicken pox. I've done some of my best coaching walking off at the end of practice with a player to discuss some current event, from a play on the field to his family or his favorite basketball team. During the off-season the best part of my day comes at noontime, when I go downstairs to our weight room to work out. There's always five or six players there, and I'll pick up on the latest lingo and music—it keeps me young. Then I'll put on a disc of *my* music —Fats Domino, Little Richard—and quiz the players on who's singing. They'll roll their eyes, but it's always something to talk about.

Jimmy Johnson once said that knowing the people who work for you is more important than knowing all the mechanics of the job, and I couldn't agree more. To motivate people you need to find out what makes them tick. You have to predict how they'll respond in tight situations, so you'll know who should get called on and who might find the pressure too great. And the players need to understand my personality, as well. If they don't, they might take my abrasiveness personally; it could drive them into a shell.

Effective managers don't direct from afar. They ask about their people's vacation plans. They join them for lunch in the employee cafeteria or corner coffee shop, find out who the smiling faces are in those photos on the partition walls.

None of these things have a direct bearing on the work you do together—until you face some high-tension crunch and find out that those relationships are what's tiding you over.

To be honest, the main reason I spend time with my players is because I enjoy it so much. When I first came to New England, everybody shut up when I entered the locker room: *There's the boss.* But now it's more comfortable, like it was in New York, and they just go on the way they were. They've come to trust that our relationship isn't adversarial. We have a common interest, after all: We both want the player to succeed.

Over the years, some of these players grow on you, till they're almost like your children. You see them play hurt. You watch them lay their bodies on the line to win, and you get emotionally attached to them. I don't mind showing my affection; there's a lot of hugging on my teams. Or I'll be telling them how proud I am after a hard-fought win, and I'll start to cry—it's happened more than once.

That said, I've never liked the term "player's coach." I consider myself a communicator, not an accommodator. I have no insecurity about getting close to a player and having to put the hammer down if he messes up or crosses the line. But even then I try to respect his dignity.

I remember my final game as a high school quarterback. It was our big match of the year, our Thanksgiving Day rivalry, River Dell versus Bergenfield. It's a scoreless tie, and we've driven the ball down to Bergenfield's 4-yard-line. I see the defense pinching in for a goal-line stand, so I call a pitch play to our halfback outside. It's a walk-in touchdown—but the guy drops the pitch, and the defense recovers.

As I trudge back to the bench, Tom Cahill calls out, "Parcells, get up here!" He puts his arm around me and we're facing the field, with all the parents and friends behind us. And Coach Cahill says, "Parcells, you SOB, if we get down there one more time and you pitch that goddamned ball, you're gonna finish your career with your fat ass on the bench." It's a hard lesson, but you couldn't tell that from the stands—as far as my mother could see, he's giving me "encouragement."

After we win the game, 7–0, Cahill comes to me in the dressing room. I'll never play for him again, but he isn't through coaching. "Why did you run that pitch—why didn't you hand it off instead?" he says. "It's not like you to do something like that." But he's *teaching* me now, not dressing me down. He's repairing our relationship, doing some damage control.

I learned two things from that incident. First, you will never see a Bill Parcells team pitch the ball near the goal line —I've told Bledsoe to disregard that play if I send it in, because he'll know I've gone completely crazy.

Second, whenever I lose my temper with a player, I never let him leave without assessing the damage. You're never too big to admit that you're wrong. There was a recent Patriots game when Myron Guyton—a player I like tremendously, and brought in from New York—didn't realize he was involved in a punting situation, and left us with only ten men on the field. When I found out, I called him a very bad name, more in frustration than anger. But Myron heard me, and he took offense; we had a strong exchange right there.

A few minutes later, right on the sideline, I went to him

and said, "Myron, you know I care, and it was wrong for me to say that, and I'm apologizing right now. But I want you to put it away, quick." He looked at me and said okay, but I didn't leave it there. After the game I stopped by his locker and teased him with the very same name. He laughed and I laughed, and that's when I knew it was over for sure.

WHEN ORGANIZATIONS CONTAIN STRONG RE-LATIONSHIPS, THEY CAN WEATHER INTERNAL STORMS.

A customer service manager gets into a loud argument with one of her reps over a botched order fulfillment. If the two people involved know and like each other, the fallout is minimal. But if they are relative strangers, each side will have to wonder what the other's anger means—and how it may affect their future work together.

Winning is something I strive for and enjoy, and it's the standard by which I'm judged. But winning isn't my life. It doesn't erase my sense of morality. It doesn't control the human part of me that responds to others.

People don't get injected with painkillers in my locker room. I've had players sneak out and do it elsewhere—Lawrence Taylor did that twice when he had a broken ankle and wanted to play—but I don't condone it. I don't consider this any major moral issue; in most cases, playing with painkillers won't cause any lasting damage. But I think my team does better with a healthy substitute than with a starter who needs a shot to play. And even if that weren't so, I wouldn't ask a player to do something I wouldn't do with my own kids. I don't want them to think that I would ever compromise them.

We have the same policy on anabolic steroids. When I hired my strength coach in New York, I told him he'd be fired in five minutes if I ever heard him recommend the stuff. I know that steroids are hard to police, and that labs create masking agents to stay ahead of the testing system. But I also know that we've seen four cases of cancer among our former Giants players, and all four of those people used steroids. Two of them are dead. I can't prove a direct link, but I'm not willing to let our players take the chance.

Over time your players become a product of your system. If you provide a way to train that's healthy and structured and gives them the results they need, they eventually buy into it.

We take a hard line, as well, on unnecessary roughness— on the vicious cut blocks and chop blocks that could end an opposing player's career. I want my team to hit hard but clean, and it's got to be between the whistles and between the lines. Once a player is out of bounds, we don't hit him; after the whistle blows, we don't hit him. There are two or three outlaw coaches in this league who encourage cheap shots, but they're not especially successful. You'll find that they lose a lot of games from unnecessary penalties.

MORE OFTEN THAN NOT, THE WAY TO WIN IS ALSO THE RIGHT _WAY._

10.

SELF-DISCIPLINE

MY FATHER SPENT MOST OF HIS WORKING LIFE WITH THE U.S. Rubber Company, now known as Uniroyal. He wound up as director of industrial relations; it was his job to negotiate contracts with the rubber workers, and to deal with any strikes, which were common in those days. When a crisis hit he'd go off for two or three weeks at a stretch, working twenty-hour days to hammer out an agreement. He saw a lot of foolishness at the bargaining table, by both union and management, and our family would hear about it later at the dinner table. "Never discount stupidity as a factor," he once told us, "because it's always in there somewhere."

Mickey Corcoran pounded the same lesson into his high school basketball players. Mickey saw stupidity all around him on the court—in defenders who wouldn't stop the ball on the break, or who'd get beaten on the baseline—but he wouldn't tolerate it on *his* team. His team would be smart, poised, disciplined. "You can't play for me if you play like that," he'd warn us. "If you want to play your own game, go join some schoolyard team."

There was a game my sophomore year where I scored about fifteen points in the first half, and our team was up by seventeen. Then I got into an argument with a referee—there was some problem with the game clock—and I drew a technical foul. Just like that, Mickey pulled me out of the game. The other team cut into our lead, till it was down to three points with two minutes to go, but my coach wouldn't even look at me. At the end we lost by one, and I'm still the invisible man.

The next day Mickey kicked me out of practice. The day after that he did it again: "You're not worth the 2 points you cost us on the technical." On the third day he said, "Are you willing to play on my terms? If you get another technical, you're not going to be on my team anymore."

I never talked back to an official again. Thirty years later, my football players know that I'm the only guy on our team who can yell at the referee—and if I go too far (which is rare), it's their job to calm me down and stop me.

"Let those other teams have the temper tantrums," I tell them. "You be the team that walks away from that punch, that won't hit the guy out of bounds, that doesn't berate the official."

FINDING A WAY TO WIN MEANS AVOIDING WAYS TO LOSE.

There are people in the NFL who contend: "Just get me the best athletes, and I'll win." I don't see it that way. I'd be the last person to question the value of athletic talent—but by itself, talent won't win for you. Unless those gifted people pay attention to detail, unless they function with intelligence and self-discipline, unless they can deal with mental pressure and perform on a consistent basis, you're not going far. Houston and Minnesota were both more talented than Denver in the late 1980s, but it was Denver that got to the Super Bowl.

I really believe this: *The team that makes fewer mistakes will generally get the opportunity to win, even when the opposition has more talent.* You may not be able to take advantage of that opportunity on a given night, but you'll have your chance. The disciplined team has to get *beaten* by somebody; it refuses to beat itself.

When my team assembles for our weekly meeting on Monday, I'll talk about a blunder that cost some other team a game that weekend. I want them to file it away, so it won't happen to us. Goal-line fumbles are obviously disastrous, but there are other, more insidious errors that will just as surely lose the game.

On my teams, eliminating penalties is a very high priority. Penalties are *always* the player's fault, unless the coaching staff is so late in sending in its play that we get a delay-of-game. Penalties reflect one of three things: a lack of concentration (offsides); a lack of judgment and discipline (holding, clipping, pass interference); or a lack of self-control (taunting, personal fouls). All are correctable; all are avoidable. I won't tolerate any of them.

Everyone makes mistakes from time to time, but a player who repeatedly gets flagged is holding his teammates back. If a guy can't stay on side—if he can't listen to the snap count on offense, or watch the ball on defense—at some point you'll have to replace him with someone who can.

The year before I came to New England, the Patriots racked up 1,051 yards in penalties, the most in the league. They'd also allowed sixty-six sacks and had turned the ball over forty-two times. Any one of those elements would keep you from winning consistently. Put all of them together, and you've got a team that goes 2-14.

Common sense told us that we'd have to improve in these areas to make it possible to win. So we brought officials into our practices, to call penalties just as they'd be called in the games. We drilled it into our players that they had to shape up. In 1993 the Patriots were penalized for only 468 yards, the least in the NFL.

At the same time, we simplified some of the multiple blocking schemes which had robbed our offensive linemen of their confidence. In 1993 we cut our sacks allowed by almost two-thirds, to twenty-three.

We still have too many turnovers, mainly because we're playing a young quarterback who's learning on the job. Drew Bledsoe threw twenty-seven interceptions last year; if our team is to get to the next level, he'll have to cut that number in half.

I make a distinction between mental errors and physical errors. Mental errors reflect poor concentration or inadequate preparation. A physical error can also result from poor concentration; if a running back carries the ball loose, fails to put it away, he's more apt to fumble. But physical errors are typically caused by an athletic mismatch, where you're up against someone whose ability is greater than yours. In team sports you have to minimize these errors—it's not like boxing, where the dominant fighter will simply knock the other guy out in a round or two. You have to figure out a way to contain the superior athlete so that he doesn't disrupt your team into losing.

Say you're a cornerback pitted against Jerry Rice, one on one. What can you do to give yourself the best chance to compete? You have to decide *where* you're going to let Rice catch the ball. You know you can't play this man everywhere on the field on everything he does, but you're certainly capable of playing him on half the field, or on most of the things he does.

You're not letting him catch the quick slant pass inside; that's too easy for the quarterback to complete. And you can't let Rice run deep on you, because that's a touchdown. That leaves the sideline patterns, the outside routes for short to moderate yardage, and that's what you'll give up. But even here you have a strategy. Since those sideline patterns involve longer throws, you'll have more time to catch up and react; if the ball's not thrown perfectly, you might be able to strip it. Or you might get there a little late, but your momentum will allow you to give Rice a good shot and knock the ball loose. Plus you have the sideline to help you. . . .

It's like a basketball team that plays against the Orlando Magic. Nobody stops Shaquille O'Neal one on one, so you put in your double teams to take something away. Maybe you'll concede Shaq his turnaround jumper, but you'll have a second guy ready to impede his move to the middle for a dunk.

It's possible that O'Neal will hit his jumper that night, and you'll still lose, but you won't have given the game away for lack of disciplined effort.

THERE IS ALWAYS A WAY TO COMPETE, EVEN AGAINST SUPERIOR FORCES, BUT IT REQUIRES STRICT ADHERENCE TO A CALCULATED PLAN.

Say you represent a medium-sized firm that's made a formal offer to merge with a complementary business—and then finds itself competing with a larger corporation that's going in for a hostile takeover. Taking advantage of its deeper pockets, the bigger company is dangling a price to the target firm's shareholders that is marginally higher than your best offer.

But that doesn't mean you've lost the war. It means that you need to convince the target company's managers—and through them, the stockholders—that you're offering a better deal, the bid price notwithstanding. You need to point out that your rival has a track record for gutting the companies it swallows, for firing rafts of employees to turn a quick buck. And you need to demonstrate that your superior compatibility will lead to higher profits for everyone down the road.

When such plans work, and seemingly lesser organizations win out, they get hailed as overachievers. If you really look at what they've accomplished, though, you'll find that they've done a myriad of things in a superior way.

Our 1986 Giants had an offensive line we called "The Suburbanites." One guy was a lawyer during the off-season, a second was a stockbroker, a third owned a growing car dealership in New Jersey. They all had those fluffy-looking faces— they looked like their mothers used to drive them to school in a station wagon. I'd say that three of the five were in the bottom half of the NFL for physical talent, at least when they came to us.

But as a group, the Suburbanites were formidable. Next to quarterback, offensive line is the most intricate job in football. You have to deal with the varied plays called in the huddle, and then the audibles based on changes in the defensive front. You have to coordinate all of this with the guy next to you, and with the five-man unit as a whole. The Suburbanites always covered for one another, erased each other's mistakes, helped out on mismatches. They excelled because they were outstanding communicators. And they were remarkably durable. For three years they stayed together without missing a game or practice.

I think durability is a kind of discipline by itself. There are players in this league who resemble those horses known as morning glories—the ones that run blazing fractions in their workouts, but get scratched when it's time to go for the money. The most valuable commodity in football is a player who can stay on the field. It takes more than luck to remain injury-free; it demands consistent training, and the discipline to avoid overextending yourself, or putting yourself in hazardous positions during a play.

Of course, the ideal situation is to have a talented team with high-level discipline—a thumbnail sketch of our 1990 Giants. Our '86 team was more dominant, and won by bigger scores, but that '90 team was mentally the best group I've ever coached. It was the smartest and most poised, and those players seemed to *enjoy* the closeness of their games. (Counting the playoffs, seven of our sixteen wins were by 7 points or less.)

They responded to pressure with precision, and as soon as they got the lead, the lights went on in everybody's head: We'd hold the ball on offense, and pressure on defense. Everyone was on the same page.

That offense set an all-time NFL record for fewest turnovers, just fourteen all year. And that defense was enthusiastic, aggressive, and intimidating—but also clear, composed, and analytical. At critical times in a game it refused to make the mistakes that swing 3 or 7 points and decide a contest.

What sets disciplined people apart? Here is what I've seen:

THE CAPACITY TO GET PAST DISTRACTIONS. I once had a wide receiver who was fairly productive. I couldn't fault his ability. But if this guy felt there was anything wrong—I mean anything at all—he wasn't going to do well, and it wasn't any great loss when he left us. There are players who get thrown by less than optimal conditions; they need perfect weather, a perfect playing surface, perfect health. There are other players who can't be distracted. They can play on grass, turf, or the parking-lot blacktop—the only thing they focus on is the competition.

THE WILLINGNESS TO CONDITION MIND AND BODY FOR THE TASK AT HAND. After a leader supplies the needed direction and knowledge base, it comes down to that old cliché: Who wants it more? Which side is prepared to push itself forward and seize the day? In professional sports, the outcome may hinge on how much

a player's body can endure. An ill-disciplined body
makes for a weak mind.

**THE ABILITY TO KEEP YOUR POISE WHEN
THOSE AROUND YOU ARE LOSING THEIRS.** A lot of
kids we get nowadays have grown up macho. They can't
take a dirty look; they can't take a harsh word; and they
definitely can't take a slap on the back of the head from
some cheap-shot artist on the other team. But mature
players will absorb these excesses in stride, even when
they're out-and-out flagrant. I tell my players to put their
emotions on hold, to stone-face their opponents. Once the
opposition knows what you're thinking, it gains an advantage.

The same applies to any business negotiation. If you
lose your cool, no matter what the provocation, you're
giving the other side of the table a diagram on how to
push your buttons. Even worse, you may accidentally re-
veal something substantive that will hurt your bargaining
position.

On a football team, it can't be one guy who's smarter
than the other side; it has to be all eleven. Each man has to
understand what we're trying to do. If they don't have that
mentality, the game pressure gets to them. They become instinct players; they react impulsively, unpredictably. Unless
the party line's unanimous, one free spirit can ruin it for the
other ten.

Take the mail-order apparel firm that wants to go top-
shelf all the way. It buys the finest cotton available. It sets up a

state-of-the-art manufacturing plant, puts out a beautiful cat-
alogue with well-written copy. Its telephone salespeople are
well trained and congenial. Its goods are packaged securely
and with flair. But if the firm's shipping system is disorga-
nized, and the customers are getting bathrobes when they ordered golf shirts, all the other efforts are wasted.

With the Giants defense, our wild card was Lawrence
Taylor. As a rookie he was an unguided missile. His pass rush
was all speed and power, no finesse. He was frantic to make a
big play at each snap of the ball. Taylor was such a good
athlete that he could take crazy, undisciplined chances and
often get away with them; with that tremendous acceleration
of his, he could retrace his steps and compensate for a mistake, get back into coverage.

But sometimes Lawrence would get burned, and the rest
of us with him. In one of the first plays of his very first pre-
season game, in Chicago, he forgot that he was supposed to
cover Walter Payton in a man-to-man defense. When Payton
ran out in the flat and caught the ball, there was no one else
near him, and he went for 53 yards.

That play woke Taylor up. It was his first glimmer of
awareness that he couldn't just fly around helter-skelter and
expect his team to win. He had to learn our system, and fit into
it. There would be times for the dramatic gamble, but other
moments would call for sound, solid, disciplined position defense.

As Taylor's defensive coordinator at the time, I empha-
sized the *when* and the *where*. When the other team was inside
our 20-yard-line, for example, it could be suicide for Taylor to
take an inside route on his pass rush. If they managed to block

him, the quarterback would either run outside our containment for a touchdown, or buy enough time to turn the play into a street game, with the receivers free to improvise till they completed a pitch-and-catch.

"Lookit," I'd tell Lawrence, "just because you're tearing around in the most aggressive manner does not mean that you're competing at the highest level. As a matter of fact, it's to the contrary. You're rationalizing that you're doing all you can to win, but the real competitiveness comes with exercising discipline and calculating your risk."

TO REACH A GOAL AS FAST AS POSSIBLE, USE ALL DELIBERATE SPEED.

I'd compare the Taylor of those days to the golfer who gets to the eighteenth hole and has an uphill, 15-foot putt to win his match. He's thinking, *I'm not going to be short*—he considers that the aggressive, competitive approach. So he strokes the putt 6 feet past the hole and loses the match, but he tells himself, "I went for it; I did the best I could." Well, he *didn't* do the best he could. He could have gauged the speed and direction that gave that putt the best chance to drop, even if that meant he might leave it short.

Take two TV producers who pitch sitcom concepts to network executives, trying to get their stories on the air. The producers are equally aggressive and hardworking, but they have very different styles of persuasion. Producer A is patient and direct, letting the story ideas speak for themselves. Producer B is hard-sell and impassioned, and his pitches drip with hype. His favorite punch line: "You'd be really foolish to pass on this."

And Producer A gets twice as many stories bought as Producer B.

Two years ago the Patriots drafted a linebacker named Chris Slade in the second round, and you couldn't ask for a guy with more enthusiasm. Chris was in superb condition, but he couldn't go more than fifteen plays at a stretch; he'd get so intense and overloaded it just sapped him. He'd burn himself out—he was like the fighter who stands all tensed-up in his corner, gritting his teeth between rounds. I spent countless hours with this kid, talking about how to stay mentally aggressive but physically relaxed. Chris was highly motivated and well intended, but he had to learn the discipline of how to pace himself. Once he understood that, he became a far superior player in his second year.

I had a fullback, Sam Gash, who was the same way. He was intelligent and responsible, but so aggressive that he'd self-destruct. He might overrun where he needed to be to make a block, and miss the guy altogether. When he had the ball, he wouldn't gather himself, wait for the hole, explode at the right moment—he'd just smash into the pile, go until he heard glass.

I've always liked players like Slade and Gash, even when they seem like dogs chasing cars; once you channel them, you'll have a superior performer. The best example, once again, was Lawrence Taylor. You need to make quick reads and decisions at linebacker, where the pages turn fast, but you also must play within a structure. For Taylor to be great, he needed some technique. At first we had to slow him down a little to integrate the spins and feints we were teaching into his pass rush. But he learned quickly. By the middle of his first year we knew we had a special player. By the end of that year he was one of the dominant players in the league. He was still a torpedo, but now there was some calculation in the firing.

By the latter part of his career, Taylor had gained enough discipline to be put in charge of coordinating our stunts, our defensive line's deployment in passing situations. He had to grasp our game plan and ride herd over his teammates; if the rush got screwed up, he was the one I'd be talking to. He took his job seriously, studied up before each game. And you can bet that his teammates listened to him—Lawrence was a guy that you didn't ignore.

TO INSTILL DISCIPLINE IN YOUR LOOSE-CAN-NON TALENTS, TRY MAKING THEM RESPONSIBLE FOR MORE THAN THEIR OWN INDIVIDUAL PERFOR-MANCE.

11.

PATIENCE

WHEN I TOOK MY FORCED SABBATICAL FROM COACHING A FEW
years back, I got to look at football from a new perspective.
The game had been my whole life for as long as I could remember. But when I'd drop by a diner Monday morning, I saw
what the public really thought.

In that diner the NFL was a coffee-and-Danish discussion, no more and no less. There was a whole other world out
there that I'd never really lived in, where football was just
another topic of passing interest.

They tell me I've mellowed since my illness. I know I eat
better and exercise more, and I have more energy these days,
which probably makes me less irritable. I've learned to curb
my tongue, which used to be sharper. But that coach's drive is
still there—and the day it starts to go is the day I'll be getting
out of this profession, for good.

Which is a roundabout way of saying that I'm still a less
than patient man. Impatience and intolerance have always
been my worst failings, the things I need to guard against.

When something interferes with my plans for my team, I lash out. I still fight my battles on too many fronts: the media front, the staff front, the bureaucracy front, the trainer front, the player front. My assistant coaches tell me I'm at my best when I'm battling. But there are times, it seems to me, when I could just make my point and walk away. There are times when the battle's just not that important, or urgent, or useful.

Patience comes hard to people in this business. Last season I got a call from Dick Vermeil, who was mulling a return to head coaching. When he'd left the field back in 1982, Vermeil was wrung out, totally spent; he was the guy who coined the term "burnout" for football coaches. Now he was telling me, "You know, I really think I have a different perspective on the game. I'll be able to approach this a lot differently."

And I said, "Coach, when I was out, my mind worked just like yours. I thought I'd be a different guy when I came back. And when you start off you *will* be—until you lose three straight games, and then you're gonna be the same guy you always were. You'll get sick of losing, and you'll fight tooth-and-nail against anyone you think is party to it."

We're talking about something inherent in the high achievers in any organization. They simply won't accept losing; if they accepted it, they wouldn't be high achievers. And they don't take consolation from what they've accomplished in the past.

A writer named Bill Libby said it best: "It's a game that never ends. The coach cannot just show up and do a bad job . . . and hope no one will notice. He can never satisfy all; seldom can he satisfy very many; and sadly, rarely, can he even satisfy himself. If he wins once, he must win the rest of the time, too."

In 1983, my debut as a head coach, the Giants lost twelve out of sixteen games. Ten years later, in my first season with the New England Patriots, we lost eleven of sixteen.

I was older, wiser, more mature, solidly established—and I don't remember feeling any better about it.

When we lose on the road, I'll spend the plane trip home in utter solitude, regardless of who's around me. I can't explain how I feel to my staff, or my general manager, or my players. It's a misery of its own quality.

When we lose at home, I'll retreat to a chair in my kitchen or living room and sit there without a word. I'll do the same thing I do on the plane—I'll analyze and agonize over how the team fell short that day. Did I pull the wrong strategic trigger? Were my players unprepared? Why did they behave the way they did? What play did we call that might have turned the tide against us? In what phase of the game did we fall short?

I'll sit there and torment myself this way for five or six hours. I may eat or not, but I won't taste the food. I'll only get up when it's time to try to go to sleep.

And it's not like the next day wipes the slate clean. I can remember losses going back to 1964, my first year in the business, at Hastings College. On this particular Saturday we were undefeated, 5-0. We were up against Kearney State, a perennial Nebraska powerhouse that was also unbeaten. Kearney had us outmanned, but Hastings led, 20–16, with a minute and forty-two seconds left to play. We'd just stopped them on downs, and had the ball first-and-ten on our own 4-yard-line.

We lost that game, 30–20.

We couldn't get a first down to run out the clock, so we punted. We'd been a tremendous punt coverage team all year, but this time our guy missed a tackle—I can see it clearly to this day, it happened right in front of our bench—and they ran it back to our one-yard-line. Kearney scored with twenty-two seconds to go, and scored again when we muffed a lateral on the ensuing kickoff. I was twenty-four years old and I had to chew a whole pack of Tums after that.

As I said, patience was never my strong suit.

In the NFL we happen to operate in a particularly impatient environment; we've got external pressure stoking up the heat that we put on ourselves. This isn't a game anymore; it's about as big a business as there is. It's about marketing, and revenue, and a corporate identity. When I broke into the sport, it felt like we were going to the playground to find out who was best. I'm a traditional guy, and I still feel that way, but I'm also part of this demanding growth industry. These days a head coach has his own newsletter, his own television and radio show. What you *wear* becomes important, which is real challenging for me; I've never been big on Brooks Brothers.

Coaches make a lot more money than they used to, but they earn it. The demands are greater, the job security nonexistent. The days of Vince Lombardi, of NFL coaches who stayed with one team twenty years and then retired, are over. A handful of franchises are still managed with commitment and patience. But most owners today are in a hurry. They'll tell a coach, "We'll give you everything you want, but you better produce." What they mean is that they want their Super

Bowl ring yesterday, and it better damn well be on their finger by tomorrow.

It's fashionable to talk about coaches burning out these days—to look at these guys as high-strung, Type A personalities who drive themselves into the ground. But that's not what is happening, not really. It's the *environment* that's burning coaches out, this terrible impatience to get to the top. In pro sports you're either number one or nothing—if you're number two, you might as well be number two hundred. The annual attrition rate for NFL head coaches hovers around 25 percent. When a guy like Marty Schottenheimer can get the boot in Cleveland after averaging ten wins a year, you know something is upside down.

We live in an era of instant gratification. In today's business world impatience is epidemic. Quick profits are all that counts. New managerial teams are expected to pay off in six to ninth months—not with an invigorated vision or a clearer direction, but with higher dividends and stock prices and fourth-quarter profit-taking. And if the greed for those easy dollars means laying off productive people, or passing up slower-growth business opportunities, or by losing sight of product quality, so be it.

Companies have been infiltrated by "activist" stockholders who don't want to hear about the mundane realities of building a business. These people are asking just two questions:

How much money did you make for me last quarter?

How much will you make for me today?

We saw this shortsightedness in spades in the failed takeover move against Chrysler by Kirk Kerkorian and Lee Iacocca, who'd led the company till its board forced him out in 1992. As chairman, Iacocca had pushed to drive up Chrysler's stock price through costly diversifications and slick, personality-driven marketing campaigns; but Chrysler got poor marks on manufacturing quality and customer satisfaction.

Meanwhile, companies like Toyota and Honda had the patience to plow profits back into reinvestment. They also laid aside substantial cash-reserve war chests, allowing them to slash prices and gobble market share in the U.S. They didn't reward their big shareholders with dividends and buybacks. They gave them something better, more valuable—a reliable plan for continued growth, no matter what the economic climate.

The post-Iacocca regime at Chrysler has made progress by emulating that patience. (They had no real choice; they were playing catch-up ball here.) The new leaders introduced consumer-pleasing models like the Dodge Intrepid at attractive price points. They trimmed executive perks and salted away more than $7 billion as a hedge against the next down cycle.

If Kerkorian and Iacocca had had their way, they would have gutted that reserve and led Chrysler into huge, new debt —just as analysts warned about a looming slowdown in car purchases. The company's stock price would have gone up again in the short term, no doubt, but at severe damage to its financial foundation.

In this case, patience won the round, but Kerkorian is still the company's largest shareholder, and Chrysler's future remains in doubt.

As for myself, I have no complaints. This game has been great to me; no one in the history of mankind has lived better than I have. I've been able to do exactly what I wanted, and I've never left the boys' club. I have no complaints—but I do resent seeing good coaches and good people sucked dry and thrown away.

ORGANIZATIONS CAN'T IMPROVE WITHOUT SETTING THE HIGHEST STANDARDS. BUT THEY ALSO NEED TO MEASURE ACHIEVEMENT AGAINST THEIR REAL POTENTIAL AT A GIVEN TIME.

What the quick-fix guys miss is that there's a *process* at work here—there are steps you need to take to build a successful organization, and if you try to skip one you'll trip. You need to be smart and efficient, you need to show some urgency, but you can't rush. In my experience it takes a minimum of three to four years to develop the nucleus of a winning football team, and that's assuming you get the resources you need and avoid disastrous injuries. A lot of owners don't understand that process—and they've got a lot of general managers, and even coaches, for company.

The new player movement rules feed into their impatience. It's hard to build for the future when the guys you're building around are due to become free agents in three years. Plus it's harder to wait for slow bloomers to come of age; with the salary cap, you can no longer throw money at the stop-gap guys who can prop you up till reinforcements arrive or that youngster grows up. With our young players now we have to fish or cut bait.

When Drew Bledsoe was a rookie, we threw him to the wolves. We had to accelerate his learning curve, and I couldn't always nurture him along as I'd have wanted to. It was rough going at the start. Skills aside, Drew was too immature to be a professional quarterback when he got here. He'd show up sleepy-eyed five minutes before a meeting. He was like a teenager on Saturday morning—you'd look at him and think, *What can this person possibly accomplish today?*

But Drew was more capable than anyone else on location here, so it was an easy decision: I just put him in and let him play; I force-fed him and lived with the consequences. I have a goal in mind for Drew, a sense of where he should be after five years in the league, and I fully expect him to get there—but there's no way of telling exactly how and when he'll make that progress. I may harp about his interceptions, but I understand that those mistakes are part of the process, too. When you rush the process—as we tried to do when we complicated Drew's job in our playoff game against Cleveland—it backfires, just about every time.

The pace of Drew's development will depend, in large part, upon the rest of the team. Drew has a Ford right now, and he wasn't ready to drive that Ford consistently last season. In two years he'll be able to drive a Ford if he has to, but by that time we hope he'll have a Cadillac, and it'll be easy for him.

The Patriots are like a lot of rising teams with a losing history. The players are good at chasing, at coming from behind, because they're used to it. They're at the point where they don't give up; they always think they've got a chance to win. But chasing is easier than protecting a lead—protecting takes more poise and maturity. You tend to pull in your horns, to play not to lose, and if the other team makes a run at you, it's hard to regain that momentum.

There were times in New York where we could be conservative on the lead, because the team we were up against had no shot to come back against our defense. But in New England I'm more likely to keep the pressure on offensively, or to tell my defensive coordinator to play the game like we're still behind—to blitz, press, force turnovers, make more plays. And slowly, surely, I can see us getting more confident when we're ahead and being challenged.

Most of us would agree that a coach, like any teacher, will get more results with patience. That's easy with players who are trying their hardest, regardless of their skill level. It's harder with lazy players, and there's a lot of laziness in professional football. There's a lot of guys who do just enough to get by—they're like the sales rep who knows how to meet his quota and keep his job, but won't help the company do anything great. You find it from time to time in a defensive unit when the score is against them; players dial down their intensity and just finish the game. I've seen it on my own teams enough to make me sick.

When people consistently perform below their level of ability, at some point they'll have to be replaced. But even here a leader must be patient. A coach needs the discipline to keep using a lazy player *until he finds someone better*; you've got to keep the train on the track until you hire a new switchman.

I've seen a lot of coaches rush to make the point that someone can't play for them, and so they send the player away, trade him or waive him. The team takes notice, particularly if the guy was a regular, and the coach feels very good about himself, because he's sent his message loud and clear: "I'm not going to tolerate this." But two weeks later that player's backup is floundering, and the team is even worse off than before. There are some organizations in the NFL which make this mistake time after time. An example? Look around, and you'll see a number of one-time Tampa Bay Buccaneers doing quite well all over this league.

PATIENCE IS RAREST—AND MOST VALUABLE— WHEN AN ORGANIZATION IS PERFORMING POORLY. IT'S NOT ENOUGH TO KNOW WHAT CHANGES MUST BE MADE; IT'S EQUALLY IMPORTANT TO DECIDE WHEN TO MAKE THEM.

Like their players, coaches have to know when to take a chance, and when to *wait* for their chance—when a badly timed gamble might cancel an opportunity to win. Back in 1967 Tom Cahill took our Army team into battle against Stanford at West Point. Army was a top-twenty team at the time, but we knew we were outmanned. Stanford was physically and athletically far superior; three or four of its players would eventually make the NFL.

That game turned out to be just as tough as advertised. Stanford went up 10–0 in the first quarter, and we had to make a goal-line stand to keep it from going to 17–0. But then we recovered a fumbled punt, and ran an interception back to their 10-yard-line, and by some miracle we tied the score at 10 at the half.

In the second half Army did its best to hang in, but Stanford still led by four points, if memory serves, with less than three minutes to play. We had the ball on our own 39, fourth down and a yard to go. All of the assistant coaches, myself included, were pressing Cahill to go for it. We figured that we hadn't stopped Stanford all day, and that once we punted the ball we'd never see it again.

But Cahill saw the situation differently, and a lot more patiently. He knew the issue wasn't just whether we could make the one yard—and a lot of bad things can stop you, from a fumbled snap to going offside. The decision he had to make was: *Did he want the game to be decided at that time?*

The fact was, Cahill couldn't decide to *win* at that juncture; converting the fourth and one wouldn't clinch the outcome, even if we went on to score. But if we didn't make that first down, the odds were very strong that we'd lose the game. Did he want to risk the outcome on that one play?

To the booing of just about every cadet and officer in that stadium, Cahill ordered a punt. On its first play from scrimmage, Stanford gained 8 yards. On its second, it gained enough for a killing first down—but the play was called back for a holding penalty. Given that break, our defense held, and we returned the ensuing punt to Stanford's 3-yard-line. Army scored in two plays, won the game against all odds—and all because our head coach had the patience and the courage to wait.

When the press asked Cahill why he'd decided to punt with so little time left, he gave them an elaborate answer. "Our defense had been playing a *little* bit better in the second half," he explained. "We have a very good punter, and we thought we could pin them deep in their territory." He went on to enumerate seven or eight factors in his decision.

"Coach, did you think of all those things on the sideline?" one reporter asked.

Coach Cahill was a very humble guy, and he honestly replied, "No, I thought of them after I'd had about three beers at the Officers' Club."

Be that as it may, Cahill had made the correct intuitive judgment. By resisting impulse, by maintaining patience, he'd found the soundest possible path of action. As he'd often tell us, "Sometimes winning is just a matter of playing harder longer than the other team."

In business, there will be lots of times that you won't have as many resources as the people you're up against. And there will be occasions where you won't be able to function as efficiently. But patient leaders never give up. They keep trying, keep persisting. They chip away as long as they're allowed to. And by refusing a premature surrender, by avoiding the fatal blunder born of panic, they allow solutions to surface and present themselves, often in the least expected places.

THE DISCIPLINED COURSE ISN'T ALWAYS THE DARING COURSE OR THE EXCITING COURSE. IT'S THE COURSE THAT GIVES YOUR ORGANIZATION THE BEST CHANCE TO PREVAIL.

EPILOGUE

No one loves to win more than I do. That old thrill of victory still pushes me, still rewards me; I've yet to find anything to replace it.

But after three decades in a highly demanding business, I've also come to discover that winning isn't everything, nor is it the only thing. As we've said from the top, no one can win every game, or contract, or promotion. As hard as we may strive, no one wins all the time.

I find a lot of value in what I do on the football field these days. Winning is a big part of that; there's not much pleasure to be had in steady losing and underachievement. But there's another part of this feeling, the part that transcends the scoreboard—the sense of doing a job well, of standing by one's principles in good times and hard. And of holding to a vision of how an organization should be shaped, and how a game should be played.

My perfect game would be a day game, a big game, on the road with a loud and hostile crowd. I don't care about the weather or the surface, but I want to be the underdog, where my team is given no real chance to win, and there's a lot on the line in the outcome. I want to feel a high level of tension on both sides, that edge you can see during warm-ups, where you can *smell* that this will be serious business.

I want to know that my players are as well prepared as they can be—that they understand the things that will allow us to win or cause us to lose. And I want to be sure that we have the element of surprise in our arsenal, if we choose to use it.

I'm hoping the other team wins the toss and elects to receive. I want to start the game on defense if I can, where my team can play with a certain recklessness; I want the other side to be the first to have to execute with precision. And I want to stop them without a first down and then get on the board quickly—that's especially important on the road.

I want the game to be a real scuffle, where both teams realize that there won't be any winning here unless you execute very well. This game won't be sloppy. There may be some errors, but they'll be forced errors. My players won't be making the deadly penalties, the concentration and judgment mistakes. They'll be aggressive, totally involved, boiling over into a little physical exuberance from time to time—but always controlled, never flagrant.

I want to gain a measure of control, to dictate the style and tempo of play. But no matter how the game unfolds, there will be a point where a reversal of fortune is in the wind. We may have to throw back a series of assaults, relinquish and regain our lead, rise to one pivotal threat. But whatever happens, I want the more resilient team to be my team.

The scoring in this game will be moderate, something like 20–17 or 24–21. But I don't care so much about the exact score, or even the level of performance, as about the fight. It has to be a hard fight, because the hard fights are the most satisfying to win.

And to put the emotional kicker on it, the game would go to the last minute with the outcome still uncertain. And then someone on my team will do something to win it at the end— he will find a way to win.

That's the kind of game where your euphoria is greatest, where the celebration is most spontaneous. When I'm finished with coaching, those are the games that will remain most vivid in my recollection. Those are the days that I'll remember the cold or the heat, the wind and sky, the raucous sound of the crowd. And I'll remember the faces of my players, so intent and so unified, who earned that win with their sweat and blood. . . .

In 1989 we opened the season with a Monday night game against the Redskins at RFK Stadium. The score was tied with two seconds left when Raul Allegre came in to try a 52-yard field goal. It was midnight. A fog was rolling in, and there were sixty thousand people screaming like banshees. And then the kick went through the goal posts, and the clock read zero, and that madhouse was suddenly a cemetery—it was like everyone had died. As I headed across the field, I could hear my players celebrating around me and behind me in the fog, but the sound was muffled, soaked into the dead silence all around us. . . .

It was the same in that 1990 conference championship against San Francisco, except now we were down a point with four seconds to go. This time Matt Bahr kicked a 42-yard field goal, and my players went wild as that whole sea of red in the stands fell still. That game was so hard-fought, so well played, that even the officials who worked it would come up to me years later to reminisce about how great it was.

And there was one other game I must mention, the one that started it all for me. It was 1954, and I was twelve years old, and my father took me to the Polo Grounds: Giants versus Steelers, my first professional football game. We were sitting in the centerfield bleachers, behind one of the end zones. The Pittsburgh quarterback was a fellow named Jim Finks, later general manager of the Bears; they had a running back named Lynn Chandnois, and the fullback was Fran Rogel. The Giants had my guy, Charlie Conerly, number 42 in your program, and there were Alex Webster and Rosey Brown—and Emlen Tunnell, he was the ultimate man to me. . . .

I'd seen the Yankees and the Dodgers, but this was more impressive; I was in awe of the whole spectacle. It was a sunny day, and I remember the rich green of the field. The Giants were wearing blue helmets, white jerseys with red numbers, silver pants, red socks. The Steelers wore black with gold trim.

It's something I've never forgotten, those pure colors and the glory. It was something that moves me to this day, that keeps me reaching for that perfect game.

INDEX